For Tama and Cassandra Tama

Married with Careers:
Coping with Role Strain

JACQUELINE BLOOM STANFIELD
Department of Sociology
University of Northern Colorado

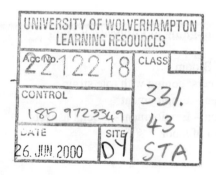
Avebury

Aldershot • Brookfield USA • Hong Kong • Singapore • Sydney

Published by
Avebury
Ashgate Publishing Limited
Gower House
Croft Road
Aldershot
Hants GU11 3HR
England

Ashgate Publishing Company
Old Post Road
Brookfield
Vermont 05036
USA

British Library Cataloguing in Publication Data

Stanfield, Jacqueline Bloom
    Married with careers: coping with role strain
    1. Married women – Employment
    2. Married women – Employment – Social aspects
    3. Sexual division of labor
    I. Title
    331.4'3

Library of Congress Catalog Card Number: 96-83249

ISBN 1 85972 334 9

Printed and bound by Athenaeum Press, Ltd.,
Gateshead, Tyne & Wear.

Contents

Acknowledgements

There are many individuals who I would like to acknowledge because this project was a direct result of their encouragement, support, and confidence in me. First, I would like to thank the members of my graduate committee at Colorado State University. Brooke R. Jacobsen introduced me to the sociology of the family; Clifton E. Barber suggested I examine role strain in the family; Edward Knop spent many hours listening to me develop my ideas on dual career couples and coping; and when he went on sabbatical Dennis S. Mileti spent many more hours with me in the conceptualization and operationalization of the dissertation. Dennis would not let me quit, and I can not thank him enough. Second, I would like to thank Ron Stanfield, my friend and roommate of more than 25 years for encouraging me to be all that I could be. Also, I would like to thank my children, Bailey and Kellin who survived having a parent in graduate school.

Preface

In the fall of 1979, at the age of 32, I entered the Ph.D. program in sociology at Colorado State University. At that time, I was a faculty spouse, the mother of a five-year old daughter and a three-month old son, and used to being a stay-at-home wife and mother. The first two years of my graduate program were uneventful. I took two classes each semester at times that worked into my husband's schedule so that he could be home with the children. I spent weekends at the library and afternoon nap times in the study.

Then, in the fall of 1981 everything changed. I applied for and was selected for a graduate teaching assistantship in the department. All of a sudden I was expected to be at school for the classes I was taking, the classes for which I was the teaching assistant, for office hours, seminars, and meetings. That meant arranging babysitters and carpools and not being home to do all the things I had done as the stay-at-home wife and mother. It seemed as if there were not enough hours in the day to do everything that had to be done, and as a result some things did not get done very often. My graduate program was going well, but home life was suffering -- we lived for semester break!

One course in my program changed the way I looked at my life and introduced me to my major research interest -- role strain in dual career couples. The course was in advanced family relationships, and one of the requirements of that course was that we research a dependent variable related to family relationships. This was my first graduate course in the family, and there were so many dependent variables to choose from that I consulted the professor. The professor suggested that I look at role strain in the family (I guess he knew I was experiencing it), and I did.

The first article I read was Rapoport and Rapoport's 1969 article on the dual career family. I read that article over several times because I realized that not only would this be the topic for my research paper and but also that I was experiencing role strain along with many others. My initial research on wife/mother role strain in dual career couples led to my dissertation on alternative dual career couple styles of coping with role strain which has led to this book *Married With Careers: Coping with Role Strain.*

1 Setting the stage

We shall understand families when we understand how they manage the commonplace, that is, how they conduct themselves and interact in the familiar everyday surrounding of their own households (Kantor and Lehr, 1975, p. ix)

The American family and social change

The family and change

Levitan and Belous posed the question, "What's happening to the American family?" in 1981. The answer they said is that the American family is changing, adapting, and evolving. They cite many statistics and draw many graphs to illustrate such changes in the family as divorce rates, number of children, and women working. The empirical study of the family is not a recent phenomenon. In fact, researchers began studying the family in order to understand some of the changes in the family that resulted from the Industrial Revolution (Yorburg, 1983, p. 8). One of the major changes in the American family resulting from the Industrial Revolution is the changing role of women (Levitan and Belous, 1981, p. viii; McNall and McNall, 1983, Ch. II; Yorburg, 1983, p. 36; Huber, 1973, pp. 1-4).

The traditional role of women in the frontier family of the Great Plains was very restricted to home-oriented tasks (McNall and McNall, 1983, pp. 23, 273). She ran the household, kept the financial books, taught the children, and so on. However, in the 1900s, increases in technology and the development of agriculture as an industry encouraged families to move from the farm to the city. This greatly changed the role of women since their lives were no longer restricted to the home.

1

Women have always contributed to the family's economic resources (Aldous, 1981, p. 117). But, with more industrialization women began working outside the home and began acquiring their own independent income. As women became less economically dependent on men, husband/wife relations became more egalitarian allowing the wife to become even more involved with activities outside of the home (Yorburg, 1983, p. 25; Goode, 1964, pp. 75-76.)

The changing role of women includes not only graduate education for women but also careers for women (Yorburg, 1983, p. 116). It was during World War II that women were recruited from the home to the labor force while the men were away. As a result, women began to question their traditional role because they discovered they could fulfill two roles -- wife/mother and employed person -- at the same time. Also during World War II, colleges, universities, and trade schools opened their doors to women and in the 1960s reliable contraceptive devices became widely available to women (Levitan and Belous, 1981, p. viii). Contraceptive devices allowed women to plan their pregnancies and thus their labor force participation or career involvement.

The dual career couple

The dual career couple is one result of the changing role of women. A dual career couple is a couple in which both husband and wife pursue careers and maintain a family life together which may or may not include children (Rapoport and Rapoport, 1969, p. 9). The US Bureau of the Census reported that in 1982 there were 7.1 million dual career couples out of 49.6 million couples (US Bureau of the Census, 1984, p. 1). Prior to 1982, there were no reports of dual career couples (US Bureau of the Census, 1977, p. 28). In fact, only 16 percent of wives in the 20,034,000 dual earner couples had graduated from college (US Bureau of the Census, 1977, p. 33).

The difference between a dual career family and a traditional nuclear family consisting of a breadwinner husband, housewife, and children is that a dual career family must operate without a "wife" (Rapoport and Rapoport, 1969, p. 8); i.e., without a person who stays home to manage the home and care for the children. The practical problem facing the dual career family is that neither the husband nor the wife is home during the day to take care of those activities which traditionally were taken care of by the women (Hoffman, 1977, p. 645). These activities include such things as child care, shopping, cleaning, and errands. Each dual career couple somehow manages to get these activities done in addition to fulfilling career role expectations.

2

The American family and role strain

Every person plays more than one role, and sometimes these roles have competing role expectations attached to them. Role strain is "the felt difficulty in fulfilling role obligations" (Goode, 1960, p. 485). Role strain can result when a person's competing role expectations are salient simultaneously, and in this type of situation role strain becomes the common state of affairs.

Role strain, as a concept, has been researched for many years. The seminal literature states that role strain or role conflict results from multiple-role obligations which the role player cannot fulfill (Stouffer and Toby, 1951, p. 395; Getzels and Guba, 1954, p. 164; Sutcliffe and Haberman, 1956, p. 695; Goode, 1960, p. 485). These researchers approached role strain both theoretically and methodologically.

Role strain is normal because "the individual's total role obligations are over demanding" (Goode, 1960, p. 485) and is the felt difficulty in fulfilling role obligations. The individual's problem, therefore is to reduce role strain, and Goode sees two ways of doing this. First, individuals can manipulate their role structure; that is compartmentalize life, delegate responsibility, and eliminate role relationships. Second individuals can adopt techniques for affecting the role bargain or negotiation they make or carry out with others. In other words, Goode accepts role conflict as normal, and says that the total role system of the individual is unique and over demanding. Individuals cannot satisfy fully all demands, and must move through a continuous sequence of role decisions and bargains by which they attempt to adjust these demands. A common thread in the role conflict and role strain literature is that role conflict or role strain is most always seen as the result of some occurrence. That is, some event happens, and this causes role strain for the person involved.

Family role strain

The family is one arena in which role strain and stress may occur. In fact, there are four major streams of research regarding families under stress (Hansen and Hill, 1964, p. 783). One stream is medical-psychiatric research which realizes that "patients have families" and that role strain or conflict exists between patients and their families. A second stream of research is the study of the problem family. A problem family is a family that is prone to crisis or frequent conflicts in the community. This is a difficult kind of research because it is often difficult to decide whether the "problem" belongs to the family or to the community.

A third stream is disaster research. Prior to 1964 (Hansen and Hill, 1964, p. 73) it was a platitude in disaster research that family roles determine what a person will do during and after a disaster. However, more recent research (Mileti, 1985, p. 21) indicates that family roles are not the most important thing influencing what a person will do in a disaster. The most important factor influencing role performance in a disaster is the amount of training a person has and whether an actual disaster emergency plan exists in the community. Disaster research studies the relationship of the family to the community, and appears to focus on the community (Hansen and Hill, 1964, p. 783).

The final stream of research is the seminal sociological studies of family crises (Hansen and Hill, 1964, p. 786). Since the turn of the century, sociologists have conducted research on the family. With the Great Depression of the 1930s, sociologists were really able to study the whole family in relation to society (Angell, 1936; Cavan and Ranck, 1938; Koos, 1946). Burgess (1947, p. 1) said that one aspect of the family which needs to be researched is the area of conflicts and crises because an unsolved conflict tends to be converted into a tension which is more difficult to treat. The three crises which threaten to disrupt the family are change in status, loss of family members by departure, divorce, desertion, or death, and conflict of members in the conception of their roles. The latter of these crises is one of the major reasons for role strain in dual career families (Stanfield, 1985, p. 362). Adaptability or flexibility of the family is the one attribute of the family that allows it to meet and overcome the crises of social change (Angell, 1936, p. 17).

Hill's ABCX model (1958, p. 43) of studying the family under stress/strain takes into account four factors: A, the stressor event; B, the family's crisis meeting resources; C, the family's definition of the stressor event; and X, the crisis itself. These four variables interacting with each other give the conceptual framework for a family under stress or facing role strains. Hill's model focuses on pre-crisis variables or the stressor event which occurs and then causes role strain, while McCubbin and Patterson's (1981, p. 9) Double ABCX model focuses on both pre-crisis and post-crisis behavior and makes the leap into coping strategies.

Dual career couple role strain

A dual career couple faces strains as a result of both spouses having careers and no "wife". Rapoport and Rapoport (1969, p. 29) say that a major problem faced by dual career couples is role strain. As Goode (1960, p. 485) says, one person can fulfill only a limited number of role obligations; when a person cannot fulfill all of his/her role obligations, role strain results.

Actually, role strain is normal in a modern industrial society like the United States because an important feature of modern social life is that

4

individuals are members of many different social groups (Killian, 1952, p. 309). Therefore, as noted in the popular press (*Wall Street Journal*, 9/19/78, p. 1; 9/7/84, p. 27; 9/19/84, p. 30; 9/28/84, p. 31; 9/16/86, p. 30) as well as in academic or scholarly works (most notably Goode, 1960, p. 485; Hunt and Hunt, 1982a, p. 500; Hall and Hall, 1979, p. 12; Holahan and Gilbert, 1979, p. 451), both men and women play multiple roles and as a result of the competing demands on their time feel role strain. The situation becomes even more complicated when individuals in dual career couples try to combine and balance their family roles and career roles. This leads to role strain in the family.

Most dual career couple role strain research focuses on the wife in the family because of the assumption that she is the one adding a primary role and therefore most affected. Determinants of wife/mother role strain fall into one of two categories.[1] The first deals with strains caused by the role expectations of the career woman; the second with strains caused by those of the wife/mother. These two categories overlap, and it is the overlap of the two sets of role expectations that causes the strain felt by the wife/mother in regard to the four role strain determinants of time management, division of household labor, child care, and perceived guilt (Stanfield, 1985, p. 356).

Time management refers to how the wife/mother organizes her time to fulfill all of her dual role obligations (Rapoport and Rapoport, 1969, p. 8; Hall, 1972, p. 471; Herman and Gyelstrom, 1977, p. 320; Johnson and Johnson, 1977, p. 392; Bryson, Bryson and Johnson, 1978, p. 68; St. John-Parsons, 1978, p. 33). Strain occurs when she cannot fulfill all of the obligations. For example, the career oriented wife/mother may have a conference scheduled, but on that day her child wakes up too sick to go to school or to child care. Role strain occurs because the career woman has to determine which has the higher priority -- the conference or the sick child.

The old folk expression, "Behind every successful man there is a woman" refers not only to the emotional side of the relationship but also to the whole complex of domestic support activities for which the wife/mother traditionally is responsible (Rapoport and Rapoport, 1969, p. 8). In the dual career family, the career woman usually has no domestic back-up for such emergency family situations as the sudden sickness of a child.

Strains caused by having to fulfill multiple role obligations are faced by the wife/mother (Hall, 1972, p. 471). Role strain results because she has to reduce her role activities selectively so that she can fulfill what she feels are the most crucial obligations. Hall (1972, p. 473) contends that women in dual career families will experience strain because their multiple roles are likely to be salient simultaneously and simultaneous role demands require setting priorities.

5

Men and women who are full-time members of the labor force continuously experience role overload (Herman and Gyelstrom, 1977, p. 321). Role overload and role strain are a function of the number of social roles held for both men and women and a function of the position (of the career) and role responsibilities.

Many women feel that their maternal role is a full-time job and that a woman who adds the role of a career will have difficulty coordinating various time demands (Johnson and Johnson, 1977, p. 392). The strain of multiple roles increases in relation to family size (Bryson, Bryson and Johnson, 1978, p. 68), and wives with two or more children feel they do not have enough time for their professional activities because of the presence of children.

One other aspect of time management has to do with partners arranging their schedules to accommodate each other (St. John-Parsons, 1978, p. 33). When schedules are not coordinated, strains occur because neither parent, especially the mother, is home to oversee domestic activities or arrange for social activities.

A second determinant of role strain in dual career families is the division of labor in the household, or who does what to ensure that the household operates smoothly and efficiently (Rapoport and Rapoport, 1969, p. 9; Epstein, 1971, p. 559; Berman, Sacks and Lief, 1975, p. 246; Weingarten, 1978, p. 45; St. John-Parsons, 1978, p. 33; Holahan and Gilbert, 1979, p. 455; Yogev, 1981, p. 869). Yogev (1981, p. 869) sums up quite well the findings of the other researchers when she says that wife/mother role strain is alleviated because of two contradictory patterns: namely, that the women perceive their husbands in a way that assumes egalitarian relationships when in fact the women actually assume most of the responsibility for household management.

The wife/mother in the dual career family has major responsibility for household management (Rapoport and Rapoport, 1969, p. 9; Epstein, 1971, p. 55; Weingarten, 1978, p. 44; and St. John-Parsons, 1978, p. 33). According to Rapoport and Rapoport (1969, p. 9) "the degree to which a couple aspire to a high standard of domestic living is a determinant of role strain for the wife/mother". This high standard refers to standards of cleanliness, food preparation, and social activities. For the traditional type of family in which the wife/mother is home during the day, these activities can be accomplished with more or less ease. However, for the wife/mother in the dual career family, role strain results because she often fulfills the traditional role at home even though she does not have the daytime hours for it.

Epstein (1971, p. 55) studied marital partners who were also law partners and determined that wife/mother role strain was alleviated because the wife/mother assumed the traditional role of the woman both at the office and

6

at home. In fact, many of these career woman lawyers had their offices at home so that the wife/mothers could fulfill all of their dual role obligations. All of the dual career wives in this study indicated their husbands were aware of the role strain encountered by the women but that the husbands did no significant amount of the household chores.

Weingarten (1978, p. 50) analyzed work and role overload of women in dual career families as a determinant of the amount of role strain experienced by the women. The wife/mothers in her sample felt they were responsible for 50 percent or more of the household management activities. In effect, the husbands may "help" with the housework, but the wife/mother retains the major responsibility and adds a second primary role to her life.

St. John-Parsons (1978, p. 33) discovered that the wife/mother in a dual career family experienced role strain because she accepted the traditional role at home but not in her career. That is, even though her husband might "help" at home with minor repairs, she accepted the responsibility of cleaning, cooking, caring for the children, vacation planning, and shopping.

Holahan and Gilbert (1979, p. 452) and Berman, Sacks, and Lief (1978, p. 246) addressed the issue of household division of labor somewhat differently. Holahan and Gilbert (1979) determined that some wife/mothers have been able to lessen the amount of role strain they experience by having husbands who are supportive of their careers to such an extent that they take an almost equal role in managing all aspects of the household. The wife/mothers have both a satisfying relationship with their husbands and achieve satisfaction from their career roles which lessens any role strain they may feel.

In contrast Berman, Sacks and Lief (1975, p. 246) concluded that the wife/mother begins to experience role strain when the two professionals are both engaged in their practices. It is at this time that the career woman begins to acquire economic independence, and the strain occurs for the wife/mother because her relations with her husband change. She is no longer a helper to her husband, but she is a co-worker and is unavailable to manage the household activities.

Therefore, based on the review above, it is the wife/mother who assumes the responsibility of seeing that the household runs smoothly and efficiently, and, as a result, she generally feels role strain.

A third determinant of wife/mother role strain in dual career families has to do with various aspects of child care. In fact, the main determinant of wife/mother role strain is the presence of children (Rapoport and Rapoport, 1969, p. 11; 1971, p. 530; Epstein, 1971, p. 561; Johnson and Johnson, 1977, p. 393; St. John-Parsons, 1978, p. 33; Bryson, Bryson and Johnson, 1978, p. 67) because raising children takes an enormous amount of energy and time. When the mother who has traditionally taken care of all aspects of child care and child rearing has outside pressures from her career, she experiences role strain.

Rapoport and Rapoport (1969, p. 11) state that the area of child care presents special problems. The couples in this research were very concerned about the possible effects on their children resulting from their dual career lifestyles. The wife/mothers indicated more role strain than the husband/fathers because child care traditionally is women's responsibility and she had to make adequate child care arrangements.

Further analysis of their data allowed Rapoport and Rapoport (1971, p. 530) to conclude that children do not suffer from having a mother engaged in a career and that in fact mothers can feel good, i.e., not strained, because their children exhibit qualities of independence and resourcefulness.

Epstein (1971, p. 561) concluded that each wife/mother lawyer in her sample was able to fulfill her dual role obligations but with strain being involved. The women interviewed by Epstein about the incompatibility of their roles, i.e., role strain, indicated that even though they felt strained, they managed to be good mothers and lawyers at the same time.

Johnson and Johnson (1977, p. 393) concluded that role strain could be identified in women in both their family situation and their career situation. However, the main reason for role strain revolves around child care arrangements and child-rearing practices.

According to St. John-Parsons (1978, p. 33) even though the family may have domestic help to ease the physical overload of household work, the wife/mother still has the emotional strain. It is the wife/mother who has the responsibility of getting the children ready for school or day care, carpooling, caring for the children on school holidays or when they are ill, and deciding which type of day care arrangement is best for preschool children.

Bryson, Bryson and Johnson (1978, p. 70) state that wives in dual career couples bear a disproportionate share of the burden for child care and that family size is a key determinant for wife/mother role strain. In these families, traditional sex roles still appear to be the basis for allocating child care responsibilities.

A final determinant of wife/mother role strain in dual career families is the amount of guilt felt by the wife/mother. Guilt is addressed by Epstein (1971, p. 560), Johnson and Johnson (1977, 394), Weingarten (1978, p. 51), and St. John-Parsons (1978, p. 39). They agree that if the demands and pressures of a person's commitments cannot all be met, role strain will result from the guilt.

Epstein (1971, p. 560) in her study of law and marital partners found that the lawyer wives in order to alleviate their guilt feelings, i.e., role strain, tried to convey the "image of a competent wife". Epstein determined that these lawyer wives experienced role strain and attempted to alleviate this

8

strain by fulfilling their household role to such an extent that they felt they had to serve homemade cakes or jams to clients. In this way they tried to remove their perceived sense of guilt at their family not matching the image portrayed as the ideal of society.

Johnson and Johnson (1977, p. 394) indicated that the wife/mother in a dual career middle class family holds middle class values which result in more time consuming child rearing practices. These time consuming child rearing practices, such as trying to reason with children, take time away from the other role obligations of the wife/mother. This in turn leads to guilt or anxiety on her part and that causes role strain.

Weingarten (1978, p. 51) concluded that most of the mothers she studied felt guilty about the time they spent away from their children. The time that the wife/mothers in dual career families devote to activities with their children depends on what they want to do and what they feel they ought to do. In this way, the wife/mothers lessen their felt amount of guilt.

St. John-Parsons (1978, p. 39) discovered that women had to deal with the dilemma arising from the clash between their personal norms and social norms. Personal norms are what they feel is right and proper behavior. Social norms are what they feel people around them feel is right and proper behavior. The women dealt with this perceived guilt with individual solutions to the problem. That is, they resolved this cause of role strain in their own manner and by expressing the belief that their children would become independent, resourceful, and self confident.

**The American family and coping
with role strain**

Coping is what people do to avoid being harmed by life strains. Coping is any response to external life strains that serves to prevent, avoid, or control emotional distress, and there is a distinction between resources and responses individuals have in regard to coping (Pearlin and Schooler, 1978, pp. 2-3) . Individuals have social resources and psychological resources available to use in developing responses to strain, and responses are what individuals actually do in reaction to a strain or problem.

There are three major types of coping (Pearlin and Schooler, 1978, p. 6). The first type of coping is responses that modify the situation. These are the most direct way to cope with life strains and are similar to Hill's (1958, p. 143) A factor, the stressor event. The second type of coping is responses that function to control the meaning of the problem. This is similar to Hill's (1958, p. 143) C factor, the definition of the stressor event. The third type of coping is responses that help individuals manage tension, and this is similar to McCubbin and Patterson's (1981, p. 9) coping factor. Pearlin and

Schooler (1978, p. 7) state emphatically that coping is not a unidimensional behavior. Coping functions at a number of levels, and is attained by a plethora of behaviors and perceptions.

Family styles of coping

Three questions emerge from the structure of coping with regard to the family. First, how do members use the resources available within their family to cope? Second, how do families use resources from outside their family to cope with stressful life events? And, third, are there differences among families in their use of internal versus external coping strategies (Olson, McCubbin et. al., 1983, p. 135)?

There are several approaches to the answering of these questions. There has been an increased interest in coping strategies of families (McCubbin et. al., 1980, p. 1) because of the changing view on stress and strain. Traditionally, family stress was seen as dysfunctional to the family, but the current view is that stress and strain are prevalent and that understanding the family coping styles is necessary to discover why some families are better able than other families to cope with strain.

Pearlin and Schooler (1978, p. 4) examined the coping strategies families used when faced with problems of marriage, parenthood, household economics, and occupational goals and activities. The three coping responses they identified are responses that modify situations, responses that help individuals manage tension, and responses that are used to reappraise the meaning of the problem. Coping becomes a process of achieving a balance in the family because as the severity of problems increase and as families experience other changes and stressors, they adapt and cope. Therefore, a family strategy of coping is progressively modified over time and involves the management of various aspects or dimensions of family life simultaneously.

Reiss and Oliveri (1980, p. 432) coined the term family paradigm which they used to refine a model of family coping in order to measure a family's intrinsic adaptive capacities and then used those measurements to predict the family's response to stress. Their point is that they should be able to predict a family's strategy or style of coping if they know the family's paradigm. Family paradigm refers to the family's social construction of reality; i.e., the family has a definite perception of reality and this perception colors the way the family sees the world and reacts to it.

Olson, McCubbin et. al. (1983, p. 136), highlight three basic themes in the research and theory about coping. First, coping is a lifelong process with no beginning or end point and can occur at the individual or family level. A second theme deals with coping efficacy, the ability of coping behaviors to reduce the causal impact of the stressor event upon the

10

definition of the event as a crisis. The third basic theme in coping research is the shift from individual to family coping.

Researchers struggle with the notion of family coping. The definition of family coping (Reiss and Oliveri, 1980, p. 431) is that family coping occurs when the family is called upon to exert unusual effort to observe, to experience, to define, to understand, and to take some kind of special action so that it can return to the more orderly routines of family life.

The shift from individual to family coping has brought a new dimension to the study of family coping styles. Reiss and Oliveri (1980, p. 432) interject the importance of the subjective reality of the family. The interactional nature of coping has become important too, along with the compromise and coordination required in the family. In effect, family coping is viewed as more than the family's responses to a stressor. Family coping is viewed as a set of interactions within the family and transactions between the family and the community.

Another way of approaching the topic of family styles of coping is to focus on coping with the conflicts between professional and parental roles like Hall (1972) does. Hall (1972, p. 474) postulates three strategies of coping with role conflict in his study of the role behavior of college-educated women. Type I is structural role redefinition; Type II is personal role redefinition; and Type III is reactive role behavior.

Gilbert, Holahan, and Manning (1981, p. 420) combined Hall's Type I and Type II coping into a role redefinition strategy, and their other strategy is role expansion which encompasses Hall's Type III.

Dual career family coping styles

Skinner (1980, p. 478) identifies two types of coping strategies. These two types are coping strategies within the family and coping strategies involving support systems external to the family. These are identified as family coping styles; however with few exceptions the studies which have dealt with dual career family coping actually deal with dual career wife coping (Stanfield, 1985, p. 355). Poloma (1972, p. 178) outlined four coping techniques within the family used by dual career women. They are defining their situation in positive terms, prioritizing roles, compartmentalizing their roles, and compromising their career aspirations to meet other role demands.

The coping strategies involving external support systems are more legitimately family strategies. One is using money to resolve overload strain, such as hiring child care and domestic help and purchasing labor-saving devices (Holmstrom, 1973, pp. 97-98). Another is making friends with other dual career couples since this helps to validate the lifestyle (Rapoport and Rapoport, 1976, p. 316). A third coping strategy is the negotiation of work arrangements, such as job-sharing and flexible scheduling (Skinner, 1980, p. 479).

Dual career couples use their own individual coping styles because no institutionalized supports external to the family exist.

Notes

1 The research on this relatively new family pattern has been primarily descriptive and focuses on women since it appears to be the women who suffer the greatest strain. Since the research area is relatively new, the concept of wife/mother role strain is not conceptually clear. For example, the term role conflict may be used when the conceptual definition is actually that of role strain.

2 Writing the script

The dual career couple is a social phenomenon whose presence has been well-documented (Hochschild, 1989; Rapoport and Rapoport, 1969, p. 4; Rapoport and Rapoport, 1980, p. 23; Skinner, 1980, p. 473). The distinguishing characteristic of the dual career couple is that both spouses pursue careers while maintaining a family life together. Researchers explain the phenomenon of the dual career couple using the two major ideas of role strain[1] and coping. This chapter examines role strain in the context of role compartmentalization, flexibility of work schedule, household division of labor, prioritizing of time-allocation, and care for dependents.

Role strain is present and is the normal state of affairs for people in society, and the family is one area in which role strain is prevalent. The focus here is on the coping styles employed as a result of role strain in the family. This book aims to discover and to explain the different ways that dual career couples cope with role strain. However, before focusing on coping styles, a few definitions are necessary.

Definitions

The concepts of role strain, dual career couple, role compartmentalization, flexibility of work schedule, division of household labor, prioritizing, and dependents are the concepts used to discover and to explain the dual career couple styles of coping with role strain. Each of these concepts has a clear conceptual definition. Each of them also has an operational or working definition specific to this book. The conceptual and operational definitions of each are as follows.

Role strain

The conceptual definition of role strain is "the felt difficulty in fulfilling role obligations" (Goode, 1960, p. 485). Role strain occurs because a person has competing or conflicting role obligations for the various roles he/she may play. In other words, a person may experience role strain because competing role demands are placed on him/her. Two of the many roles that a person may play are employed person and family person.

The working definition of role strain says that these two roles place competing demands on the person because being employed means that one cannot be at home to be a family person at certain times. Likewise, being a family person means that one cannot be at work to be an employed person at times. Therefore, since both of these roles demand a person's presence, then at certain times the person will experience role strain.

Dual career couple

The conceptual definition of a dual career couple is a couple in which both husband and wife pursue careers and maintain a family life together either with or without children (Rapoport and Rapoport, 1969, p. 9). The working definition is virtually the same: a couple in which both husband and wife pursue careers and maintain a family life together either with or without dependents at home (i.e., children, elderly parents, or chronically ill persons).

The term "career" designates a form of work involvement that is continuous, developmental, demands a high level of commitment, and is intrinsically rewarding (Rapoport and Rapoport, 1976, p. 9). Even though careers are usually associated with business management and the professions, the concept does not coincide precisely with any specific occupational titles. A conscientious salesperson or clerical worker may treat his/her work as a career, while a burned-out executive may give only a perfunctory role performance. In actuality, the distinction between job and career is partially subjective and does not represent discrete categories of work involvement. An interesting observation about the term career is that

> "Career" is in itself a masculine concept (i.e., designed for males in our society). When we say "career" it connotes a demanding, rigorous, preordained life pattern, to whose goals everything else is ruthlessly subordinated -- everything pleasurable, human, emotional, bodily, frivolous .... (Slater, 1970, p. 72).

14

Perhaps it is careers and not women's participation in the labor force that is incompatible with family life (Hunt and Hunt, 1982 p. 503). In other words, the problem is not that women are working outside the home; the problem is that women are pursuing careers and are embracing the masculine characteristics associated with careers. In effect, the married dual career couple both are "sociological men" and as a result men are becoming "sociological women" (Hunt and Hunt, 1982, p. 49).

Role compartmentalization

The conceptual definition of role compartmentalization is the ability to distinctly separate roles (Rapoport and Rapoport, 1969; Epstein, 1971; Bryson, Bryson and Johnson, 1978; Hall and Hall, 1979). The working definition relates role compartmentalization specifically to the two roles of employed person and family person. Role, compartmentalization is the ability to focus on home and family when at home and to focus on work while at work. In other words, if a person is not able to compartmentalize roles, that person may experience role strain because he/she spends time at work thinking about home and family life demands that are not being met and vice versa.

Flexibility of work schedule

The concept of flexible work schedule is related to role strain in the dual career couple (Epstein, 1971; Hall and Hall, 1979; Holahan and Gilbert, 1979; Poloma, 1972; Skinner, 1980), and individuals in some professions may have more flexible work schedules than individuals in other professions. The conceptual and working definition of flexible work schedule is a work schedule that permits an individual to leave his/her place of work during normal business hours for a nonwork related reason. An individual who has a flexible work schedule may experience more or less role strain than an individual with a rigid or nonflexible schedule.

Household division of labor

Conceptually household division of labor is job specialization. Operationally, each couple has its own household division of labor or arrangement of who does what to keep the household running smoothly. A household that operates smoothly and efficiently experiences less role strain than a household which does not operate smoothly (Rapoport and Rapoport, 1969, 1971; Skinner, 1980).

15

Prioritizing

Prioritizing (Rapoport and Rapoport, 1971; Skinner, 1980) is deciding that one thing or role is more important than another thing or role. By definition, the dual career couple has role strain. Therefore, the couple either individually or together has to prioritize at times because not every demand can be met.

Dependents

The conceptual definition of dependents is persons who cannot take care of themselves. The operational definition therefore includes children, elderly parents, or chronically ill family members. The presence or absence of dependents in a family is related to role strain because dependents can be very demanding. For example, child rearing takes an enormous amount of time and energy which may conflict and compete with career role demands (Rapoport and Rapoport, 1969, 1971; Epstein, 1971; Johnson and Johnson, 1977; St. John-Parsons, 1978; and Bryson, Bryson and Johnson, 1978) as does a chronically ill family member (Venters, 1980; Cleveland, 1977).

Dual career couple style of coping

Coping is any response to life strains that serves to prevent, avoid, or control emotional distress (Pearlin and Schooler, 1978) and the disruption of mutually supportive social relations. There is no conceptual definition of dual career couple style of coping. However, the working definition is that a couple style of coping is a description of how the dual career couple actually combines their work roles and home roles; i.e., how they cope with role strain.

There is a general consensus that these concepts/variables are very important issues in the dual career family. Theoretically, therefore, these concepts/variables are important, and the study of them is instrumental in determining couple coping styles.

Theoretical Model

The members of a dual career couple may perceive varying degrees of role strain in fulfilling the competing demands of two of the roles they play, i.e., professional person and family person. This book does not attempt to measure role strain in any way. This book examines the family contextual factors of dependents, role compartmentalization, schedule flexibility,

16

household division of labor, and prioritizing as they relate to couple style of coping.

There are a limited number of ways that a couple can deal with these contextual factors. The family can use an internal coping technique. Internal coping techniques are those which are internal to the family or which exist within the family. An example of internal coping is defining the role strain situation in a positive manner. In other words, the family can decide that the children are learning independence and social interaction skills during their long days at day care centers rather than suffering from parental neglect. This is what Reiss and Oliveri (1980, p. 431) call the family paradigm or the family's subjective definition of the situation.

There are other possible internal family coping techniques. Parents can prioritize their roles. In other words, the parents can decide which role -- spouse/parent or employed person -- has priority over the other role. Depending on which role has priority, the spouse/parent may compromise some career aspirations or assume the "super person" role of doing everything.

According to Hall (1972) one may either personally redefine roles which would be an internal coping strategy or structurally redefine a role which would be an external coping strategy. External coping techniques are the second basic type of coping strategy a family may adopt. Examples of external coping include employing domestic help to relieve the burden of household chores or negotiating work arrangements so that a more flexible work schedule allows for time during the day for nonwork-related activities.

Therefore, this book assumes that role strain exists and that there are different ways that couples cope with it. Identifying and defining these different ways is what the rest of this book is about.

Purpose of the book

The purpose of this book is to typologize and describe how dual career couples cope with the competing demands of home life and careers. In doing this, the book answers the question: How does the dual career couple cope with role strain?

As stated above, the American family is in a state of change, and some traditions, i.e., the traditional family of a breadwinner husband, stay-at-home wife, and children, are changing. In the past during periods of social change or when traditions were changing, social philosophers like Emile Durkheim, Karl Marx, or Max Weber stepped forward to study society and to offer explanations and solutions to societal problems. Today, sociologists step forward to study society and interactions in society and to provide accurate and reliable information about social life that is based on observation rather than intuition, speculation, or impression.

This book is a descriptive sociological study of how dual career couples cope with role strain. The unit of analysis is the couple, specifically the role relations between individuals in couples. The objective is to determine how the couple affected by role strain manages its everyday life while experiencing role strain.

Several issues are addressed in answering this question about how dual career couples cope. First is the issue of developing a conceptual definition of dual career couple styles of coping with role strain. Second is the issue that even though couple style of coping is not conceptually well-defined, role strain, role compartmentalization, division of household labor, flexibility of work schedule, dependents, and prioritizing are. This book develops a typology of couple styles of coping with role strain that addresses these issues.

Notes

1 There is some confusion regarding the term role strain. Some researchers use the term strain, others use conflict or incompatibility (Burr 1973, p. 120, 131). All, however, are referring to the difficulty in fulfilling role demands.

3   What the players said

This chapter outlines the different dual career couple styles of coping with role strain. This is a two step process. The first step is to use descriptive statistics to show how the couples answered the questions (see Appendices for Interview Schedule and Measures) relating to role strain and the indicators of coping style . The second step is to lay out the framework of the alternative ways that dual career couples cope with role strain.

The data

Role strain

Role strain had three dimensions. These dimensions were role strain at home (intra-role), role strain at work (intra-role), and role strain due to the competing demands of home and work (inter-role). Couples were questioned about all three dimensions of role strain and were scored either high or low.

On the role strain at home dimension, 81 percent or 29 of the couples scored high, meaning they felt difficulty in fulfilling all of their role obligations at home. Seven or 19 percent of the couples scored low, meaning they felt only slight difficulty in fulfilling all of their role obligations at home. On the role strain at work dimension, 64 percent or 23 of the couples scored high meaning they felt difficulty in fulfilling all of their role obligations at work. Thirteen or 36 percent of the couples scored low meaning they felt only slight difficulty in fulfilling all of their role obligations at work.

On the third role strain dimension, the dimension of most interest to this book, role strain due to the competing demands of home life and careers, 14 percent or five of the couples scored high meaning they felt difficulty in fulfilling the competing demands of home life and careers. Thirty-one or 6 percent of the couples scored low meaning they felt only slight difficulty in fulfilling the competing demands of home life and careers.

The data on role strain shows that there are two levels of role strain -- high and low -- for each dimension of role strain. High role strain at home and high role strain at work are more common than high role strain due to the competing demands of home life and careers. This means that more of the couples feel difficulty in fulfilling all of their role obligations at home and at work and less difficulty in combining their roles. Similarly, fewer couples do not feel difficulty in fulfilling their role obligations at home and at work and more feel difficulty in combining their roles.

In other words, one set of couples has high intra-role strain at home and at work and low inter-role strain due to the competing demands of home life and careers while another set of couples has low intra-role strain at home and at work and high inter-role strain due to the competing demands of home life and careers. There are two sets of couples with different levels of role strain, and each has a different style of coping with role strain. This book aims to discover and explain how these two sets of dual career couples cope with the competing demands of home life and careers.

Role compartmentalization

Role compartmentalization also had two main dimensions and was defined as the ability to separate roles. One dimension was the ability to separate work life from home life and to focus on home life when at home (home to work). The other dimension was the ability to separate home life from work life and to focus on work when at work (work to home). Couples were questioned about both dimensions and were scored either high or low.

On the home to work role compartmentalization dimension, 14 percent or 5 of the couples scored high. This meant that they do not think about work when they are at home. Alternatively, 86 percent or 31 of the couples scored low which meant they do think about work when they are at home.

On the work to home role compartmentalization dimension, 28 percent or 10 of the couples scored high meaning they do not think about home when they are at work. Conversely, 72 percent or 26 of the couples scored low on this meaning they do think about home when they are at work.

In addition, both the home to work dimension and the work to home dimension of role compartmentalization had subcategories of questions. For both dimensions, couples were asked why they think about work at home and why they think about home at work.

Couples gave a total of 44 responses when asked why they do not home to work role compartmentalize, i.e., why they think about work when they are at home. These 44 responses divided unequally into four reasons. One reason given was the nature of work; e.g., "I always keep in mind that I have patients in the hospital because I might be called to the hospital at any time". Out of 44 responses, this type of reason was given 34 times or 77 percent of the time. Another reason given was the lack of time at work to do everything; e.g., "I'm too busy at work to think about work". Out of 44 responses, this type of reason was given 14 times or 9 percent of the time. A third reason given was we enjoy our work; e.g., "I think about work when I'm home because I enjoy my work". Out of 44 responses, this type of reason was given 3 times or 7 percent of the time. The final reason given was dependents; e.g., "One of us stays home every morning with the baby". This type of reason was given 3 times or 7 percent of the time.

When they are at home, some couples spend a lot of time thinking about work because a characteristic of professional life is that "the job is personally involving".

We don't separate home and work mainly because our work is such that we can work at home. Our lives are integrated .... We write and publish articles together, and use each other as a resource. This enriches our married life (Couple 11).

Every time the phone rings, it could be patient related -- the hospital or the answering service calling about a patient. We've adjusted to being on call, but ... get frustrated when he's gone all the time (Couple 16).

There are so many little things that can go wrong in our profession that you constantly worry about it. We use each other as a sounding board and this gives us new ways to think about things. This strengthens our relationship because it gives us one strong area of interest to talk about (Couple 35).

We do paper work at home. We each have our own office and patient files at home, so every night we get out the files we need for the next day.... We set rules for clients: no calls at home and no suicide. Clients are supposed to use the answering service, and then we have the choice of whether or not to call them back. Occasionally, a client will call at home, and that's a real invasion of our private time (Couple 34).

> We try not to talk about work because it's depressing. We're in the same department and this puts stress on us because I'm considered "his wife" instead of a professor and person in my own right. When we start talking about this, we just end the conversation (Couple 13).

Couples do not home to work role compartmentalize because the nature of their work is such that it carries over into nonwork hours either because of phone calls, thinking about cases or clients, or just because they enjoy talking about work. Similarly, couples do not work to home role compartmentalize, i.e., think about home at work, because "work isn't my life".

When couples were asked why they do not work to home role compartmentalize, i.e., why they think about home when they are at work, they gave a total of 35 responses. These 35 responses divided unequally into five reasons. The reason given the most was the nature of home life; e.g., "home is an enjoyable part of my life". Out of 35 responses, this type of reason was given 18 times or 51 percent of the time. Another reason given was the nature of work; e.g., "When my train of thought is disrupted at work for some reason, I think about home." This type of reason was given 6 times or 17 percent of the time. Dependents was the third reason given; e.g., "The kids call me at work if they need a ride somewhere". Dependents were given as a reason 4 times or 11 percent of the time. Vacation was the fourth reason given; e.g., "I get brochures at the office about professional meetings in exotic places, and I call her to see if she can get away from her office then". Vacation was given as a reason 4 times or 11 percent of the time. The final reason given was the lack of time during the day at home; e.g., "There's not enough time during the day to do everything". This type of reason was given 3 times or 9 percent of the time.

> Actually, I have a pet peeve about those people who split their lives into private and professional. It's all one life, just different, interlocking spheres (Couple 34).

Couples were asked two other questions about work to home role compartmentalization, i.e., thinking about home when at work. One question dealt with how they fit thinking about home into their work day, and the other asked for an example of what home-related thing they might think about or take time to do during their work day.

When asked how they are able to think about home when at work, couples gave a total of 32 responses. These responses divided unequally into three reasons. The reason given the most times was the nature of work; e.g., "My time is my own unless I'm in class or a faculty meeting is scheduled". This type of reason was given 17 times or 53 percent of the time. Another reason given was we just do it; "You don't interrupt work because some things are always in the back of your mind". This type of reason was given 3 times or 44 percent of the time. The final reason given was we plan; e.g., "We plan our kids' appointments and activities far in advance, write them on the calendar, and plan the rest of our schedule around that". This type of reason was given one time or 3 percent of the time.

When asked for an example of a home-related thing they might think about at work, couples gave a total of 15 responses. These responses divided unequally into six reasons. The examples and their percentage and frequency of response are: dependents (e.g., "I think about my daughter getting to Brownies after school") 40 percent or 6 times; vacation (e.g., "going on vacation") 33 percent or 5 times; dinner (e.g., "what we'll have for dinner) 13 percent or 2 times; household maintenance (e.g., "the plumber") 7 percent or 1 time; and commuting time (e.g., "the long drive to and from Denver") 7 percent or 1 time.

Couples gave a total of 23 responses when asked for an example of a home-related thing they might do during their work day. These responses divided unequally into four activities. The examples and their percentage and frequency of response are: make phone calls (e.g., "about our new house") 48 percent or 11 times; leave work for errands (e.g., "take the cleaning") 22 percent or 5 times; leave work not for errands (e.g., "play racquetball") 22 percent or 5 times; and other (e.g., "talk to my adult daughter about her sick child") 9 percent or 2 times.

> The good thing about academic life is that you can do some of your work in the evenings or on the weekends, so you can do other things during the day ... like go home to see if the cleaning lady closed the door because last time she forgot (Couple 3).

> I just do it. I think about our house in Vermont when the job stress get bad. That's why we have the house -- it's our safety valve (Couple 32).

> Well, sometimes I block off time on my appointment book, but more likely I'll see that I have a free hour and I'll go do something that has to be done during the day, like going to the bank (Couple 22).

> I don't abuse the privilege of flexibility. But I have to go back at night a lot or on the weekend or do something on my lunch hour; so when I want to take off early for some reason, I just do (Couple 12).

From the data regarding role compartmentalization, therefore, it appears that more of the couples do not compartmentalize their lives, i.e., more scored low on the variable, than do compartmentalize their lives and that they have a variety of reasons for their behavior. The essence of role compartmentalization deals with the ability of couples to affect their role strain due to the competing demands of home life and careers (inter role strain) by making them feel that they are fulfilling the role obligations and demands of each of their roles. The data show that some couples have low role strain from the competing demands and low role compartmentalization; i.e., they do not feel difficulty fulfilling their competing role demands and they do not compartmentalize their lives. Similarly, the data show that other couples have high role strain due to the competing demands of home life and careers and high role compartmentalization; i.e., they feel difficulty fulfilling their role demands and they compartmentalize their lives.

Household division of labor

A third concept of major interest is household division of labor, or who does what to keep the household running smoothly. One way of accomplishing household chores is to pay someone else to do the chores, i.e., by using a cleaning service and/or lawn service, or eating at restaurants to avoid the chore of cooking meals and cleaning up. Couples were questioned about these.

Cleaning or yard service was used by 56 percent or 20 of the couples on a regular basis while 44 percent or 16 of the couples do not pay anyone else to do their household chores. Eating dinner out at least once a week was one way that 67 percent or 24 of the couples used to keep their household running smoothly while 33 percent or 12 of the couples never ate dinner out. On the other hand, 39 percent or 14 of the couples indicated that they never carry in already prepared food for dinner while 61 percent or 22 of the couples did carry in already prepared food for dinner at least once a week.

In addition, couples were asked to give an example of a chore that they hired out. There were a total of 38 responses to this question which divided unequally into five categories of examples. The examples, their percentage and frequency of being given, were: Housecleaning (e.g., "laundry") 39 percent or 15 times; yard work (e.g., "rototilling") 18 percent or 7 times; home maintenance (e.g., "carpentry") 18 percent or 7 times; other (e.g., "everything" 16 percent or 6 times; and none, 8 percent or 3 times.

These data indicate that over half of the couples do pay someone else to keep parts of their household running smoothly and they could give a variety of examples of how. This is using someone external to the household to keep the household running smoothly. Even those couples who hire outside help for some things have a certain number of household chores to do, i.e.,

24

laundry, grocery shopping, or financial planning. The couple respondents were asked about a series of items and could score either high or low. A low score means a low division of household labor or that only one person in the household does the specific chore while a high score means a high division of household labor or that two or more persons in the household do a specific chore. In some cases, the chore was hired out, just ignored by the couple respondents, or not applicable to the couple respondents.

Those specific chores for which the number of low scores exceeded the number of high scores and their respective percentages and frequencies are: vacuuming at 39 percent or 14 times versus 19 percent or 7 times; dusting at 36 percent or 13 times versus 19 percent or 7 times; laundry at 64 percent or 23 times versus 31 percent or 11 times; daily trash at 64 percent or 23 times versus 31 percent or 11 times; weekly trash at 83 percent or 30 times versus 14 percent or 5 times; clean toilet at 47 percent or 17 times versus 8 percent or 3 times; clean bathtub at 44 percent or 16 times versus 11 percent or 4 times; mow and water lawn at 67 percent or 24 times versus 19 percent or 7 times; plan meals at 72 percent or 26 times versus 22 percent or 8 times; grocery shopping at 61 percent or 22 times versus 39 percent or 14 times; car maintenance at 50 percent or 18 times versus 28 percent or 10 times; arrange for sitters at 28 percent or 10 times versus 3 percent or 1 time; pay bills at 69 percent or 25 times versus 31 percent or 11 times; and take care of pets at 42 percent or 15 times versus 36 percent or 13 times. In other words, of the 18 specific chores, 78 percent or 14 of the chores were scored as low division of labor items, meaning that only one person in the household does the chore.

Those specific chores for which the number of high scores exceeded the number of low scores and their respective percentages and frequencies are: make beds at 36 percent or 13 times versus 33 percent or 12 times; clean up dishes at 61 percent or 22 times versus 39 percent or 14 times; make social plans at 56 percent or 20 times versus 42 percent or 15 times; and financial planning at 58 percent or 21 times versus 31 percent or 11 times. In other words, of the 18 specific chores, 22 percent or four of the chores were scored as high division of labor items meaning that two or more persons in the household share the chore.

Another way of approaching the division of household labor is to see the degree of internalness which exists within the homes of the 36 couples. Of the 36 couples, 86 percent or 31 scored low on division of household labor degree of internalness while 14 percent or 5 scored high. Therefore, regardless of the way that division of household labor is approached the data show that low division of household labor is more common than high division of household labor.

All of the couples were questioned in more depth about their internal household division of labor. They were asked why they divide the

25

household labor up the way they do, how they decided to do it that way, how it is working out, and for an example of how they share a specific chore.

When asked why they divide the household labor up the way they do, couples gave a total of 40 responses. These responses divided unequally in five categories. The first category is equality, e.g., "not fair for one person to do everything". This type of response was given 35 percent of the time or 14 times. Another category is likes and dislikes, e.g., "loathe housework". This type of response was given 28 percent of the time or 11 times. A third category is level of tolerance, e.g., "He's more picky". This type of response was given 19 percent of the time or 4 times. Another category is traditional male/female work lines, e.g., "At our house we have men's work and women's work". This type of response was given 8 percent of the time or 3 times. The final category of responses is other, e.g., "We do all our own chores because we maintain separate residences". This type of response was given 29 percent of the time or 8 times.

When asked how they decided on this household division of labor, couples gave a total of 39 responses. These responses divided unequally into five categories. The first category is family circumstances, e.g., "She has regular full-time employment". This type of response was given 46 percent of the time or 18 times. Another category is premarriage agreement, e.g., "Before we got married we decided he would stay home with the kids". This type of reason was given 18 percent of the time or 7 times. A third category is the way we were raised, e.g., "learned household responsibility when I was growing up". This type of reason was given 18 percent of the time or 7 times. Another category is concern over female economic independence, e.g., "We keep our money separate because I want her to know how to manage it if I die". This type of reason was given 19 percent of the time or 4 times. The final category is result of previous marriage, e.g., "We were both married before and we learned from earlier experiences that you have to share". This type of reason was given 8 percent of the time or 3 times.

When asked how they think their household division of labor is working out, respondents gave a total of 36 responses. These responses divided unequally into two categories. The first category is satisfactorily, e.g., "It keeps our relationship more romantic because we can buy presents for each other with our own money". This type of response was given 89 percent of the time or 32 times. The other category is not satisfactory, e.g., "We would like a wife at home". This type of response was given 11 percent of the time or 4 times.

Finally when asked for an example of how they share a specific chore, respondents gave a total of 37 responses. These responses divided unequally into two categories. One category is do together, e.g., "Each morning we each make our half of the bed". This type of response was given 57 percent of the time or 21 times. The other category is do separately, e.g., "We take turns by the week fixing dinner. The one who cooks also plans the meals and shops. The other one cleans up the dishes". This type of response was given 43 percent of the time or 16 times.

When you get married you are supposed to share. Even though I'd rather sit down and read the paper after dinner, I don't; I feel obligated to help clean up. When she first started working, when the kids were older, the one of us that was home would take care of things -- get the kids places, fix dinner, you know all those kinds of things. It's working out fine now, but we used to make a job jar -- write all the chores on a slip of paper and you do the chores you pick for a week (Couple 12).

She has a lower threshold for cleanliness than I do, and she keeps the bathroom really clean.... I started taking care of the plants and I get mad if she re-waters them.... Basically, we share the housework 50-50, but we're gone all day and eat out every night so it really doesn't get too messed up. We spend about an hour on Saturday morning cleaning up (Couple 13).

We maintain separate residences [in different states] and we both have maids. I [wife] loathe housework and knew as soon as I had enough money I'd pay someone else to do..., I [husband] don't have time to do it myself and she [the maid] knows how to do it. We both feel housework is a waste of our time and we never want to waste our time together doing chores unless it's something fun like planting a garden (Couple 33).

She got her job first, it's regular employment. I'm working out of the house and generally have the baby all day while she's at work. I have no expectations about doing any work while the baby is awake, but the situation is getting better. Soon the baby will be old enough for day care, and I'm interviewing for jobs. The situation might reverse itself.... (Couple 8).

We share the household chores because it's a way to spend time together and because we both feel we do more than our share. If we formally divide it up, we feel better about it.... Our division of labor kind of evolved over the years. We definitely want to raise our child in an atmosphere with nontraditional mommy/daddy jobs. We were intellectually in agreement about this before we met, and now we practice it.... It would be nice to have a wife at home, a live-in housekeeper.. It would be a loss of privacy and we'd probably have an intellectual problem about having a slave, but it sure would make our life easier (Couple 23).

We bought into the traditional roles we learned from our parents. I thought I'd be superwoman after we got married, but I realized I couldn't do it all. I suggested we hire Merry Maids and he agreed. It's working out really great -- I don't worry about cleaning and that keeps the stress down (Couple 28).

We were both married before and spent some time living without a spouse. As a result I had to learn how to do some things around the house -- I had 7 kids. She had 2 kids and her own way of doing things. Now we have a cleaning lady to do what we don't want to do, and that's really great ... but we do make our bed together every morning, it's huge! (Couple 26).

Whoever hates it the most doesn't do it. We both hated the burden of fixing dinner every night and decided the only fair thing was to divide it up by weeks. One week I cook and he cleans up. The next week he cooks and I clean up. The one who cooks also plans and shops for that week, and it's such a relief to know you only have to do it for a week. When necessary we can switch, because it's really all negotiable (Couple 4).

First of all, we keep our money separate. I'm financially responsible for my son and I was poor so long that I don't really trust anyone else with my money.... The house is the framework for the family; there's a sense of community in the house, and that's really great. We sat down before we started living together -- we're married now -- and worked out a cohabitation/marriage contract dealing with child issues, money, possessions, and credit cards. There was nothing in the contract about sex or housework.... There's a real sense of community around here (Couple 34).

Household division of labor is an important issue for couples, and they have different ways of dividing it up and different reasons for the way they do it. From the data, it appears that low household division of labor is more common than high household division of labor and the data also show that household chores have a relationship to role strain.

Flexibility of work schedule

A fourth concept of major interest is flexibility of work schedule, that is, being able to leave work during the day for nonwork-related reasons. There were two dimensions to flexibility of work schedule, and the first dimension was flexibility in regard to dependents. A high score on this dimension meant that a couple could leave work during the day for a dependent-related reason. A low score on this dimension meant that a couple could not leave work during the day for a dependent-related reason. In regard to dependents, couples were asked if they could take their dependent(s) to health care appointments during their (the parents) work day or if they could take their dependent(s) other places during their (the parents) work day.

In response to the ability to take dependents to health care appointments, 82 percent or 14 of the couples scored high and 18 percent or 3 of the couples scored low. Similarly, in response to could they take their dependents other places, 71 percent or 12 of the couples scored high and 29 percent or 5 scored low.

The other dimension of flexibility of work schedule was flexibility in regard to other nonwork-related reasons. Couples were scored either high or low on this dimension. Of the 36 couples, 69 percent or 25 were scored high meaning they can leave work for nonwork-related reasons. On the other hand, 31 percent or 11 of the couples were scored low meaning they could not leave work during the day for nonwork-related reasons.

Her job is really much more flexible than mine. I really couldn't take off for anything unless it was an extreme emergency.... I reschedule my appointments for the day.... (Couple 18).

We set our schedules far in advance and write everything on the calendar. Otherwise, the one who is most available takes care of it (Couple 34).

We spend a lot of evenings and weekends on work, so we just take off if we want to go someplace or if the kids need to go someplace. We both have the flexibility to rearrange our work schedules to fit our needs (Couple 3).

The three days a week that I'm in Denver, he does everything. Takes care of the kids, cooks, cleans, and does errands. Fortunately his schedule at work is such that unless he's in class he can leave (Couple 10).

Before he was born, work was my number 1 priority; but I made a conscious decision when I was pregnant that I would always put him

[son] first, and I have ... rescheduled meetings and appointments to do things with him (Couple 31).

Neither of us can leave work, we depend on our sitter for everything (Couple 25).

The work day is flexible to the extent that time can be blocked out on the appointment book, even though a medical emergency may call me back to the office (Couple 16).

The data indicate that in regard to flexibility of work schedule, the majority of couples do have flexible schedules. In other words, they can leave work during the day for any reason, and this ability to leave work affects the way couples feel about how they are combining their roles.

Prioritizing

There were two dimensions to prioritizing. One dimension, prioritizing chores at home, was deciding what things at home to do given the time constraints. Couples were scored either high or low on this dimension. The other dimension of prioritizing was deciding which role, family person or career person, was most important. Couples were scored either high or low on this dimension also.

On the chores at home dimension of prioritizing, 72 percent or 26 of the couples scored high meaning that both ignore chores while 28 percent or 10 of the couples scored low meaning that they ask for (or hire) help in completing chores. On the roles dimension of prioritizing 56 percent or 20 of the couples scored high and 44 percent or 16 of the couples scored low meaning that more give priority to the career person role and less give priority to their family person role.

Couples were questioned further about prioritizing in regard to chores at home. They were asked why they prioritize, how they prioritize, what kinds of things they might do if they had more time at home, and for an example of how they have prioritized. A variety of responses were given to each question.

When asked why they prioritize, couples gave four categories of responses. The categories and their respective percentages and frequencies are: prioritize (e.g., "react to what has to be done the next day and get ready for it") 74 percent or 28; hire help (e.g., "hire someone to do what we don't want to do") 16 percent or 6; superwoman complex (e.g., "She'll do what I don't do") 8 percent or 3; and dependents (e.g., "child takes priority") 3 percent or 1.

30

Three categories of responses were stated when couple respondents were asked how they prioritize. The categories and their respective percentages and frequencies are: home (e.g., "do it when it has to be done") 69 percent or 25; fun (e.g., "do what we want to do") 17 percent or 6; and work (e.g., "work has top priority") 14 percent or 5. When asked what they might consider doing if they had more time at home, responses fell into five categories. The categories and their respective percentages and frequencies are: hobbies (e.g., "read") 33 percent or 14; home maintenance (e.g., "organize") 30 percent or 13; spend time with family (e.g., "spend time together") 16 percent or 7; nothing (e.g., "Look for something to do away from home.") 14 percent or 6; and spend time with friends (e.g., "entertain friends") 7 percent or 3. Finally, couples gave four categories of responses when asked for an example of a time they had prioritized. The categories and their respective percentages and frequencies are: family (e.g., "read to kids") 39 percent or 15; work ("grade papers") 26 percent or 10; leisure (e.g., "plant garden") 26 percent or 10; and other ("go shopping") 8 percent or 1.

Couples were also questioned more about their prioritizing of roles. They were asked why they choose one role over another, how they are able to do it, and for an example of a time they chose either their family person role over their career person role or their career person role over their family person role.

When asked why they chose one role over the other, couples gave a total of 38 responses which divided unequally into three categories. The categories and their respective percentages and frequencies were: work has priority (e.g., "slighting work affects many people") 58 percent or 22 times; home has priority (e.g., "being a good wife is more important than being a good attorney") 21 percent or 8 times; and it depends on the situation (e.g., "Do one with greatest urgency") 21 percent or 8 times. They also gave three categories of responses when asked how they chose one role over another. The categories and their respective percentages and frequencies are: nature of work (e.g., "schedule is flexible") 76 percent or 28 times; plan (e.g., "a lot of planning") 22 percent or 8 times; and just do it (e.g., "Let home things slide.") 3 percent or 1 time.

When asked for an example of a time they chose one role over another, 20 of the couples gave an example of a time they chose their home role over their office role. Responses fell into four categories. The categories and their respective percentages and frequencies were: dependent (e.g., "sick child") 45 percent or 9 times; special event (e.g., "birthday luncheon with friends") 40 percent or 8 times; animals (e.g., "the vet had to come") 10 percent or 2 times; and tired (e.g., "too tired to work at night") 5 percent or 1 time. Twenty-two of the couples gave an example of a time they chose their office role over their home role. The responses fell into two categories. The categories and their respective percentages and frequencies were: nature of work (e.g., "rescheduled birthday dinner") 91 percent or 20 times; and other (e.g., "forgot Memorial Day was a holiday and already scheduled appointments") 9 percent or 2 times.

> We are constantly putting out brush fires -- things with deadlines get done first. The garden has to be planted now, but it will have to wait until I finish my grades.... I do university work 15 or so hours a day, but not 15 hours straight. I'm trying to sell my house, so if someone wants to see it I have to go home for that, but I wouldn't go home to turn the sprinkler off (Couple 33).

> I have a strong sense that day time equals work time and evening equals home time. Unless it's very critical -- like being home for the vet to check the horses -- the two don't cross.... I would lie, and have my secretary reschedule appointments because of professional reasons.... (Couple 23).

> The top priority for us is the fun stuff -- spending time together. Stuff we do at home is fun -- we hire out the housework and yardwork and only do what we want. There's never a deadline at home. There are deadlines at work that sometimes require extra work, but that's not a conflict (Couple 28).

> Work has top priority for us.... We know that any time the phone rings it could be a medical emergency that one of us will be called in on. If the phone rings, you go. Last Christmas we planned a big party -- lots of preparation went into it. Right before the guests were supposed to arrive, I got called to the hospital. She hosted the party alone and I came home two days later.... (Couple 1).

The data show, therefore, that more of the couples score high on both dimensions of prioritizing and that they had a variety of reasons and could give a variety of examples regarding prioritizing.

Dependents

Dependent was conceptualized for this study as someone living at home who is dependent like a young child would be. Dependents could be young children, chronically ill persons, or elderly parents. There were five dimensions to this measure. Couples were asked if they had a dependent living at home. Those couples who said yes were questioned further about their dependents.

Of the 36 couples, 44 percent or 16 had dependents living at home and 56 percent or 20 did not. When those couples with dependents living at home were asked if they could do as much as they would like to with dependents, 35 percent or 6 said yes while 65 percent or 11 said no.

Those couples with dependents living at home were questioned further about the time spent with their dependents. They were asked how they arrange time to do things with their dependents. There were 20 responses to this question. The responses fell into four categories. The categories and their respective percentages and frequencies were: make special arrangements (e.g., "block out time in appointment book") 40 percent or 8 times; just do it (e.g., "If emergency, just leave") 35 percent or 7 times; someone else does it (e.g., "Grandpa lives here") 20 percent or 4 times; and exchange hours (e.g., "do work after kids gone to bed") 5 percent or 1 time.

They were then asked why they thought they did or did not do as much as they would like to with their dependents. There were eight responses indicating they did as much as they would like to do with their dependents. Responses fell into two categories. The categories and their respective percentages and frequencies were: quality time (e.g., "because it's quality time") 88 percent or 7 times; and flexible job (e.g., "My job is flexible") 13 percent or 1 time. There were 12 responses indicating they did not do as much as they would like to with their dependents. Responses fell into two categories. The categories and their respective percentages and frequencies were: time constraints (e.g., "Time is so structured") 83 percent or 10 times; and work (e.g., "pressures of job") 17 percent or 2 times.

Couples were then asked how they would like to do more or less with their dependents. There were 16 responses indicating how they would like to do more. Responses fell into two categories. The categories and their respective percentages and frequencies were: do enough (e.g., "I do as much as he'll let me") 50 percent or 8 times; and activities (e.g., "sports") 50 percent or 8 times. There was one response indicating how they would like to do less with their dependents. The responses fell into the nature of children category (e.g., "baby is so demanding").

The third, fourth, and fifth dimensions of dependents were who dealt with them, what were the impacts of dependents, and how did having dependents affect your relationship, respectively. When asked who dealt with dependents, a total of 18 responses were given. Responses fell into four categories. The categories and their respective percentages and frequencies were: Parents take turns (e.g., "The one with the hour most free does it") 44 percent or 8 times; father (e.g., "I work in Denver, so he does it") 22 percent or 4 times; mother (e.g., "My schedule is more flexible") 22 percent or 4 times; sitter (e.g., "The sitter would take....") 11 percent or 2 times.

Couples were then asked about the impacts both at home and the office in regard to dependents. They gave a total of 13 responses in regard to impacts at home. Responses fell into two categories. The categories and their respective percentages and frequencies are: nature of parenthood (e.g., "No expectation about doing work at home with a baby around") 54 percent or 7 times; and nature of childhood (e.g., "demanding child") 46 percent or 6 times. They gave a total of 15 responses in regard to impacts at the office. Responses fell into three categories. The categories and their respective percentages and frequencies were: nature of parenthood (e.g., "miss child when I'm at work") 60 percent or 9 times; no affect (e.g., "doesn't") 27 percent or 4 times; and relations with co-workers (e.g., "colleagues think he's cute.") 13 percent or 2 times.

When asked how the time spent with their dependents affected their own relationship, a total of 17 responses was given. Responses fell into three categories. The categories and their respective percentages and frequencies were: negative affect (e.g., "a drain on our relationship") 47 percent or 8 times; no affect (e.g., "no affect" 35 percent or 6 times; and positive affect (e.g., "makes us closer") 18 percent or 3 times.

We don't do as much with our kids as we'd like to because our jobs require so much of our time, even on weekends and in the evening. Really we'd be a lot better off if we didn't have kids, they are kind of a distraction -- but well worth it.... They call me at work, and sometimes my office staff doesn't know me as Mrs. [X], they know me as Dr. [Y] ... really would like to take long summer vacations but I feel we do spend quality time with them (Couple 3).

There was a radical change in our lifestyle after he was born. We didn't anticipate the severity of the impact a child would have on us.... We are struggling with our nontraditional household division of labor which has become more traditional since he was born. She's [wife] more nurturant and I justify not spending so much time with him because I'm the provider.... There's conflict in our relationship, too, because of the lack of time to be together. We'd like to go away for a weekend.... (Couple 23).

Having a young child has made me more understanding of my coworkers who have kids -- sometimes you just have to miss a meeting.... We never vacation without them [the kids] because we enjoy doing things with them. We all spend so little time together regularly that we really like being together (Couple 5).

We gave up our social life to be with our kids, they are top priority.... During the academic year, there is really a lack of time to be together, but every summer we go to our summer house in Vermont. I spend the

whole summer there with the kids and he commutes every weekend --
that takes a lot of planning.... (Couple 32).

The data regarding dependents indicate that less than half of the couples had
dependents living at home and that those with dependents living at home had
a variety of comments to make about them. Having a dependent at home
influenced role strain sometimes, but not always.

Framework of alternative coping styles

These descriptive statistics identify the framework of the alternative dual
career couple styles of coping with role strain. Based on all the data
collected, there are two styles of coping with role strain. Style A of coping
is characterized by high role strain at home and at work, high flexibility of
work schedule in regard to dependents and other reasons, high prioritizing
of chores and roles, and low role strain due to the competing demands of
home life and careers, low home to work and work to home role
compartmentalization, and low household division of labor. This style of
coping is labeled *Flexies* because these couples indicate flexible work
situations which allow them to fulfill their dual role obligations with less
role strain.

Style B of coping is characterized by high role strain due to the
competing demands of home life and careers, high home to work and work
to home role compartmentalization, high household division of labor, and
low role strain at home and at work, low flexibility of work schedule in
regard to dependents and other reasons, and low prioritizing of chores and
roles. This style of coping is labeled *Rigidities* because these couples
indicate rigid, i.e., not flexible, work schedules which do not allow them to
fulfill their dual role obligations as easily as Flexies.

35

4 The flexible style of coping with role strain

The Flexible style of coping is characterized by high role strain at work, high role strain at home, and low role strain due to the competing demands of home life and careers. Couples who employ this coping style are Flexies. This chapter fills in the Flexie framework by analyzing what the couples said about role strain.

Role strain at work

Role strain at work is a fact of life for Flexies. Factors which influence whether role strain is high or low are flexibility of work schedule, dependents, work to home role compartmentalization, and prioritizing of roles. These factors are intricately related.

Regardless of whether or not dependents were living at home, Flexies had high flexibility of work schedule. Flexies perceive a tremendous amount of work schedule flexibility. They feel that they can leave work for any reason as long as they meet all specific class times or scheduled appointments. A common statement heard from Flexie academics was that my "time is my own unless I have a class or a faculty meeting". A similar statement common among health and legal professionals was either that "sometimes I see I have some unscheduled time on a day and I'll leave the office" or that "I'll just have my secretary block off time on the appointment book so I can do something else". Flexies are also not opposed to having secretaries call patients or clients to reschedule appointments. As a matter of fact, one couple, one in the health profession and the other an academic, who live life like it was a brush fire which they are constantly putting out, said

> The physical demands placed on us far exceed the physical time and energy available. So we constantly make sacrifices and decisions about where to be when. For me, the option of closing the office for a whole day or a part day is like a safety valve. The fact that I can have my secretary reschedule appointments for me -- lie for me to my patients -- so that I can get a horse ready for a prospective buyer ... (Couple 23).

Flexies perceive a lot of job flexibility. Since they do feel they can leave work during normal work hours for nonwork related reasons, they often do. While at the office, they make lists of things to do and places to go, and then leave the office to do these things. In other words, having a flexible schedule encourages low work to home role compartmentalize. If the freedom or flexibility exists to fulfill other role obligations, Flexies say, "let's do it". Flexies give two reasons for their low work to home role compartmentalizing: the logistics of life and time constraints.

The logistics of life include coordinating the schedules of all family members with job commitments. In other words, how can one person drive three children to three different places at the same time and fulfill other commitments too. In cases like this, the one with the most flexible schedule for the day does the transporting. Flexies say life takes a lot of planning, and a lot of that planning has to take place during the work day because appointment times have to be checked or changed or sometimes carpools have to be arranged. One couple, one a health professional and the other an academic, said

> ... block out time in advance on the appointment book because I like to take my kids out to lunch at least once a week... (Couple 16)

Flexies also write down on their calendars (both at home and at work) all dependents' activities and scheduled appointments far in advance because that is one method of easing conflicts between work and home. Another couple, both health professionals, employ the calendar technique because if the activity or appointment is written down already and if a colleague asks them to attend a meeting they can say no.

> The one of us who is most available takes over in an emergency situation. Otherwise, we set our schedules far in advance and write his [child] scheduled activities on the calendar. That way we plan our work around his schedule (Couple 34).

Some nonwork related errands can only be done during the day, so time constraints become an issue also. For instance, banking business can only be done during certain weekday hours and the same is true of travel planning. Flexies do things like this any time during the day. Similarly, appliance repair people only make house calls during certain weekday hours, and Flexies perceive no difficulty in being called away from their offices at these times. Another common statement heard from Flexies as to why they do not work to home role compartmentalize was, as one couple both legal professionals said, "work isn't our life, and we don't stop thinking about home just because we leave in the morning". When given a choice between a home life role obligation or a career role obligation, a Flexie will generally select the home related role.

Therefore, Flexies have role strain at work because of the interplay of the indicators of flexibility of work schedule, work to home role compartmentalization, and prioritizing of roles. They have no qualms thinking about and planning home related activities while at work or about leaving work for a nonwork-related reason and together these show that Flexies give priority to their home life role when they are at work. Flexies have high role strain at work because they often leave work during the day to fulfill nonwork related role obligations and they do not do their work at home.

Role strain at home

Another fact of life for Flexies is high role strain at home. The factors that influence role strain at home are household division of labor, home to work role compartmentalization, dependents, prioritizing of chores at home, and prioritizing of roles.

Households with dependents

A common assumption about dual career couples is that the presence of dependents living at home is the most crucial factor in determining how much role strain is present at home. Relying on that assumption, one would expect that only those couples with dependents living at home would experience role strain. However, Flexies are characterized by high role strain at home, regardless of whether or not they have dependents at home.

On another indicator of coping style, home to work role compartmentalization, Flexies are low. Flexies do not compartmentalize their dual roles. Another common assumption is that role compartmentalization for dual career couples without dependents is high. Relying on that assumption, one would expect couples without dependents to be high on home to work role compartmentalization. That is not the case. Virtually all Flexies, regardless of whether or not dependents lived at home, had low home to work role compartmentalize. Nevertheless, the indicator of dependents is useful to organize this discussion. Flexie couples with dependents have one more reason for home to work role compartmentalizing, and that reason is that they do have dependents which gives them an additional role obligation at home.

"Exhaustion rules the roost" when a baby is present, says one Flexie couple, both recent law school graduates and new parents (Couple 8). The husband conducts his law practice out of their home with the baby present while she is regularly employed in a very "relaxed" office. Because he has the baby at home all day while he is supposed to be working, he has a constant reminder of his role as parent. As a result, he has no expectations for good work during the day, and therefore stays up late for his legal work and is a "zombie" during the day.

Working at home is not specific to couples with babies. Virtually all Flexies say they work at home. A common statement heard from Flexie academics is that there is never enough time to get everything done. There are lectures to prepare, papers to grade, research to conduct, and students to help. It is a never-ending process, and Flexies seem to thrive on it. As one couple, both academics, said

> We don't leave work at the job. Our lives are integrated and we don't separate home from work. Actually, it's an enrichment for us. We publish articles together even though we are in different disciplines, and use each other as a resource (Couple 11).

Being able to work at home is especially useful when dependents are present in the household because situations occasionally arise which require that children be home from school or day care either because of illness, scheduled vacations, or unscheduled days off like snow days. One couple, both health professionals, with three children indicated that they occasionally do the "parking lot shuffle" (Couple 5) when one or more of their children is sick. In other words, they divide up the day; one stays home in the morning, then they switch at lunch time in the hospital parking lot and the other one stays home in the afternoon. Fortunately for them it is an uncommon situation. In these types of cases, the parent who stays at home can work at home, i.e., not role compartmentalize.

Sometimes the parent is working at home and the dependent does not even know it. A common Flexie statement, this one from a health professional/academic couple, was that "there are so many demands on my time, that even when I'm doing something with him [child] I'm thinking

39

about other things" (Couple 23). So, for Flexies, having dependents at home is just one more role obligation with which to deal.

In regard to prioritizing of chores at home and prioritizing of roles, households with dependents have one more variable with which to deal than households without dependents. Flexies are characterized by high prioritizing.

One Flexie couple, one a health professional and one an academic, with three preschool-age children indicated the extent of their prioritizing

> One evening she was at a meeting and I was home with the kids even though I was on call. None of my patients was scheduled to deliver, but you can never really plan on these things. Anyway, I got a call from the hospital that one of my patients was approaching transition, and that I better get there fast. There wasn't time to call my wife home or even to call a neighbor, so I just piled all three kids into the car and went to the hospital. I left the kids at the nurses' station.... (Couple 16)

Career role is of utmost importance here, and this is high prioritizing of roles. In regard to chores at home, Flexies tend to ignore things at home for which they do not have time. A common statement heard from Flexies is "there are so many demands on our time, some things have to be ignored", or "it's more important and fun to do things with kids, i.e., help them with homework or play with them, than to do chores". So, Flexie couples tend to do only the necessary and immediate chores such as people related things and chores necessary to keep people functional. Another common statement heard from Flexie couples is that "our priorities change from time to time" or "our priorities seasonally change". Flexies once again are reactive to their situation.

Households without dependents

Even without dependents, Flexies have high role strain at home. Flexies do not home to work role compartmentalize, they have a low household division of labor, and when at home they usually select their career person role over their home life role while at the same time neglecting or ignoring certain household tasks.

Role compartmentalization means being able to separate the dual roles under consideration. Flexies do not separate their roles, they integrate them. A common statement heard from Flexies, regardless of their profession, is that "the nature of my work is so demanding". One two academic Flexie couple, who teach at different universities in different towns, said

40

We conceptualize home as an okay place to work, and therefore we work at home. Our careers require a lot of thinking about and planning and since work time is highly structured we do a lot at home (Couple 31).

Another Flexie couple, one an academic and the other a health professional who is in charge of the business aspects of his private practice, said

It's my personality style. It takes me at least an hour to unwind from a day at work. I worry about the marketing strategies and other business aspects of the office more than about patients (Couple 23).

These two illustrations show the demanding nature that Flexies attribute to their careers and show that Flexies bring work concerns home with them at the end of the day.

Flexies perceive that work has a demanding nature and that they do not have time to do everything. As this Flexie couple, one a health professional and the other an academic, so eloquently said

Our lifestyle is so complex that we have to be continually integrating it. We can't separate our roles because if we did there wouldn't be time to do everything. This way we try to make time (Couple 16).

The hows and whats of home to work role compartmentalization are fascinating. In other words, when one is at home supposedly accomplishing home life role obligations, how do thoughts of work creep in and what kind of thoughts are they? Flexies say that "some things just flash through your mind or are in the back of your mind all the time". That is, the thoughts are always there; only sometimes they are more salient than at other times due to the nature of the thought. For example, if a patient calls through the answering service and is suicidal, then that patient's problem takes precedence until it is eased says a Flexie couple, both psychologists who are in separate practices but keep offices at home (Couple 34). The telephone is the major way that thoughts of work creep into home life for health professionals.

Thoughts of work also creep into Flexie households because they enjoy their work immensely and like to talk and think about it. One couple, both in the legal profession and in positions of authority at work said

We enjoy our work, and so we think about it more than from 8 to 5. This broadens our relationship because we can share both personal and professional aspects of our life (Couple 2).

41

It appears that Flexies do spend time at home fulfilling some of their career role obligations. The fact that they are able to fulfill competing role obligations influences their low role strain due to the competing demands of home life and careers (inter-role strain). In other words, Flexies do not role compartmentalize and they have low inter-role strain.

Household division of labor is another indicator of coping style for Flexies. Flexies have a low division of household labor, meaning that they do not have specific ways of accomplishing household chores. They divide their household labor in several ways. Some divide it equally, some unequally, and some hire outside help.

For those Flexies who hire outside help, the most common help to hire is a cleaning service and the most common reason for doing so is because the wife is working full time outside of the home and cannot do the cleaning. The husband in a couple who are both health professionals said that they have a cleaning service once a week because his wife works and her income pays for the service.

> Actually, there was never a discussion about it. The house was her domain. When she started working, she hired a cleaning service (Couple 1).

A Flexie academic couple echoes that sentiment. "She lacks the time and inclination to do housework, and so we pay someone else to do it" (Couple 9). The wife in this academic couple told her husband that since she was working someone else would have to come in and totally clean every week. He agreed readily.

Other Flexie couples indicated that having a cleaning service relieves them of some of the strain and distaste they feel in regard to housework. "Merry Maids keeps the stress of my not cleaning down" says the wife in a two lawyer couple. They were both brought up in traditional households with mothers who did not work outside of the home, and they fully expected to follow the roles into which they had been socialized. She struggled with cleaning and the whole superwoman ideal before admitting the futility of it. Her husband was responsive to the idea of Merry Maids and now the burden of housecleaning is eased.

"I loathe housework, and knew I'd hire someone as soon as I could afford it", says one spouse in an academic Flexie couple. This couple has a rather unique situation in that they are geographically separated the majority of the time. They maintain separate residences in separate states because they teach at universities in these states; each has a cleaning service. The husband in this couple says that he lacks the skills, which his cleaning woman has, for housecleaning.

Even those couples who hire outside help to keep their household running smoothly have to divide up some aspects of home life that are beyond the realm of a cleaning service. Some things like daily bed making are totally ignored, while other things like making social plans or financial planning are shared. To a certain extent, all of the Flexie couples divide up their household labor. Some, as already indicated, keep their households running smoothly by hiring other people to do it. The others do it themselves.

> The division of labor works well. It's not fair, but it works. She is the overall manager of everything in and about the house (Couple 3).

This couple, both academics, agree that their household division of labor is inequitable. Since he is not American and does not understand the American culture yet, there is no other way for their household to be.

"We couldn't do it any other way", says one spouse in a two lawyer couple (Couple 10). "I wouldn't be pregnant again if it wasn't working out so well with him [husband] as a househusband". There is total role reversal in this couple. Both were practicing attorneys when they met and she had three children from a previous marriage. When they got married, they agreed that he would interrupt his career and take care of her three preschool age children. They also agreed she would get pregnant, and they would start their own family. This couple illustrates the most unequal and extreme household division of labor. She does virtually nothing at home, and he does not work outside of the home at this time[1].

By far, the majority of Flexie couples feel that they share the household labor evenly. A common statement heard from Flexies was "you're supposed to share when you get married" or "it's too much for one person to do alone". A characteristic of dual career couples is that

> We're not home much and we eat dinner out every night, so the house doesn't really get messed up. We spend about an hour on Saturday morning cleaning up. There's no routine or structure to who does what; we just do it, 50/50 (Couple 13).

Flexies indicated that they were brought up learning to help around the house because in several cases both of their parents worked outside the home. A recently married legal couple who share their housework equally said

> It's the way we were raised. Both of our parents worked and as kids we were expected to help out at home irrespective of sex. I learned cooking, sewing, and ironing, and she learned about building as well as domestics too (Couple 35).

Equality between the sexes is important, and for that reason Flexies often keep their money separate. That is, they have separate checking accounts from which they pay their separate bills. They also pool some money for joint expenses such as house payments, utilities, and food expenses.

> We're each responsible for our own bills. But we keep our money separate for other reasons too (Couple 14).

This couple (above) both in the legal profession deal with the issue of female economic independence daily at work. The economic dependence of women, they say, is economically and psychologically dangerous to both men and women. Because they deal with this issue on a daily basis and have seen first-hand how dangerous it is, they want to be sure that they avoid it. The policy of separate financial statements also helps to boost a woman's credit rating and at the same time having separate money also keeps their relationship more romantic because then they can buy each other gifts with their own money.

Related to household labor are prioritizing of chores and prioritizing of roles. Flexies are characterized by low household division of labor and high prioritizing of chores and of roles. Flexies do not have a structured way of accomplishing their household chores, except for those who pay someone else to do the chores. Flexies also tend to ignore chores around the house when they are feeling pressured by the demanding nature of their careers since their common operating procedure is to do things when necessary, i.e., to react to situations as they arise. Chores get ignored because the Flexie motto at home is "work comes first when you have to make a choice." This is just the opposite of the Flexie motto at work which is "home comes first when you have to make a choice." It is hard to say, however, which is actually more salient, the role demands from work or the distaste of some home life role obligations.

Role strain due to the competing demands of home life and careers

A third fact of life for Flexies is high role strain due to the competing demands of home life and careers, i.e., inter-role strain. The factors that are relevant here are home to work role compartmentalization, work to home role compartmentalization, and flexibility of work schedule. Flexies are characterized by low home to work and work to home role compartmentalization and high flexibility of work schedule. These are the factors that impact on inter-role strain.

Flexies have flexible work schedules. They can leave work during normal workday hours for nonwork related reasons which are defined either as home life role obligations or home life demands. Since Flexies often leave their place of work during the daytime hours which are normally considered work hours, they often bring work home for the evening or for the weekend. In other words, Flexies do not role compartmentalize either at home or at work because they see their dual roles as different spheres of the same role. One Flexie couple, one an academic and the other a health professional, indicated their reason for not role compartmentalizing.

> When I get home I continue thinking about whatever I was thinking about at work. I can't shut off my mind when the big hand crosses the 12.... Neither of us has 9 to 5 jobs; we are responsible for a certain work load and our productivity is measured by the quality of our work, not when we do it, ... so one of us can leave early in the afternoon to pick up our child after school or take her places (Couple 24).

Another Flexie couple, both health professionals, agreed that home and work just cannot be completely separated since they are both on call at night. "Whenever the phone rings, it could mean going back to work" (Couple 12), they say.

Another reason Flexies do not role compartmentalize is because they perceive a lack of time both at home and at work to fulfill their competing role demands. A Flexie academic couple (Couple 3) who are in the same department at the same university illustrate this quite well. They say that some errands can only be done during the work day and they have to coordinate their children's activities and schedules with their own. Therefore, they often have to leave the office to either do an errand or chauffeur a child to activities. As a result, they continue, they feel time constraints at work because they had to leave or time constraints at home because they have to bring work home. Daily life is a circle for this couple; they lack time at work because they leave to do errands and they lack time at home because they have to finish their work which they did not do because they were doing an errand. In other words, when a Flexie is at work, thoughts of home surface, and when a Flexie is at home, thoughts of work surface.

This lack of role compartmentalization and the related flexibility of work schedule interact to give Flexies the feeling of low inter-role strain. They feel that they are fulfilling all of their dual role demands.

Flexies have learned to live with their levels of role compartmentalization and flexibility of work schedule. As a matter of fact, they have thoughts on what factors have influenced their abilities to live as dual career couples.

45

Some factors have made their lives easier and some factors have made their lives more difficult, but none had negative feelings about the dual career lifestyle.

Even though some Flexies could not identify any factor which makes being a dual career couple difficult, many could. Some of the factors which they identified as making dual career life more difficult include low monetary rewards and a perception of time constraints. The husband in one Flexie couple in which one spouse is an academic and the other spouse a health professional who work at the same university says

> Relatively low pay makes it hard. The financial reward here is not sufficient for the kind, level, and amount of service I give to the university. We can afford to both work. There are costs like her clothing, a spare car, food costs, which are all greater because she's working. Even child care when the kids were little (Couple 24).

However, by far the majority of Flexies say that what makes being partners in a dual career marriage difficult is the lack of time they feel due to the pressures and nature of their careers. A recently married, recently graduated two lawyer couple (Couple 35) say that going to work every day and being separated for at least eight hours a day after spending all of their time together in law school makes it hard for them. Also, she says, making the decision to start a family is hard because of the

> ...intense nature of our profession. It would be hard to be out of the profession for any length of time; plus I would worry about how the kid would fit into our schedule. He [husband] had chicken pox and was really sick, and I felt bad leaving him at home alone. How would I feel if it were a child? (Couple 35)

Flexies indicate that they have been "programmed to think we can do whatever we want to do", and that is why they feel a lack of time both at home and at work. A common complaint is that "we don't have enough time for each other because our work and home lives overlap so much". In fact, scheduling and trying to get everything done in a day is another factor that makes it hard for Flexies.

Of course, there are some Flexies who say there is nothing that makes dual career life difficult. One reason for that is, as one recently married two lawyer couple says, "We have nothing to compare it to, so we don't know any different. We've always been dual career" (Couple 28). It is much more common for Flexies to identify factors which make the dual career lifestyle easier, i.e., cooperation, understanding, and enjoyment of work are the factors which make being a dual career couple easy. In some cases, Flexies are in the same profession and therefore understand the commitments and nature of their spouse's work. Regardless, both are professionals and understand that the other has commitments.

> I have an understanding and supportive husband, and he is willing to compromise his own career and help at home. We give each other moral support. He likes me working outside the home because it makes me a more interesting person -- I have more stimulating things to talk about than just dinner and gossip (Couple 3).

This type of understanding is just as important as understanding about career demands. Flexie wives feel they are fortunate because they have both kinds of understanding not only from their husbands but also from their children and parents. Another Flexie couple, both health professionals, say that it is their mutual respect for their profession and for their spouse which is the only thing that permits them to live the lifestyle (Couple 25). They add that they had "sheer determination that we were going to do it and do it well".
Cooperation, understanding and

> I would be unhappy staying at home, and if I'm not happy, he's not happy. We were at college together, but we didn't plan a dual career lifestyle; it just happened. And we enjoy it! (Couple 9)

This Flexie couple, both academics, sum up the Flexie feeling on factors that make the dual career lifestyle easy. It is easy because they enjoy it. They enjoy the flexibility of their work schedule that lets them leave during the day and finish up their work in the evenings, on the weekends, or during vacation.
In summary, Flexies are characterized by low inter-role strain. They feel they fulfill the competing demands of home life and careers with little difficulty, and identify cooperation, understanding and enjoyment of work as factors that affect the dual career lifestyle.

Notes

1 Even though this section describes households without dependents, the discussion of this couple with dependents fits in well because of the unequal household division of labor.

47

5 The rigid style of coping with role strain

The Rigid style of coping is characterized by low role strain at work, low role strain at home, and high role strain due to the competing demands of home life and careers. Couples who employ this coping style are Rigidities. This chapter fills in the Rigiditie framework by analyzing what the couples said about role strain.

Role strain at work

Role strain at work is a fact of life for Rigidities also. Factors which influence whether role strain is high or low are flexibility of work schedule, dependents, work to home role compartmentalization, and prioritizing of roles. These factors are intricately related.

Regardless of whether or not dependents were living at home, Rigidities had low flexibility of work schedule. Work schedule flexibility was a completely subjective feeling on the part of Rigiditie couples because few of them had specific starting or ending times at work, even though their respective offices had specific hours during which they were open. An occasional late arrival at the office or an early departure from the office was not uncommon, but generally speaking the Rigiditie couples felt that their work schedules were rigid and that they should be at the office during the day regardless of other obligations.

When the issue of choosing a home life role obligation versus a career role obligation surfaces, couples who use the Rigiditie style of coping feel that without question the career role obligation has priority. One Rigiditie couple, both in health professions, indicated the inflexibility which exists for them.

> One or the other of us, and usually both of us, is always at the office and our hours are 8 a.m. to 9 p.m. The office is our source of livelihood, and we have lived like this for 30 years. It was hard for the kids when they were little to understand why both their parents couldn't attend programs at the same time (Couple 21).

Rigidities have this feeling that the office always has priority and this contributes to their perceptions of work schedule inflexibility.

Another Rigiditie couple, one a health professional and the other a legal professional, with grown children could not think of a time when they had to leave work for a home related reason. They said, "This is the way we want to be. We are both happy about our work..." (Couple 29). Some couples use the Rigiditie coping style because they want to, while other Rigiditie couples are not so satisfied. One couple, both recent law school graduates, new parents, and the only Rigiditie couple with a dependent, have trouble with the lack of flexibility they feel. They have student loans to repay which puts them in a financial squeeze and because of the baby the wife has interrupted her law career. They are rigid because he is one of the few who actually does have set work hours and a full and demanding schedule each day. He says

> My job makes us both inflexible because it has top priority for us. I want to do a good job and that means a lot of hours at the office and at home, during the week and on weekends too (Couple 18).

Rigidities have low role strain at work because the perception of inflexibility at work encourages both the compartmentalizing of roles and the prioritizing of work roles over home life roles. In other words, Rigidities do not leave work during the day and as a result feel comfortable that they are fulfilling their work demands because they have chosen to give priority to their career roles.

Role strain at home

Another fact of life for Rigidities is low role strain at home. The factors that influence role strain at home for Rigidities are household division of labor, home to work role compartmentalization, dependents, prioritizing of chores at home, and prioritizing of roles.

49

A common assumption about dual career couples is that the presence of dependents living at home is the most crucial factor in determining how much role strain is present at home. Relying on that assumption, one would expect that only those couples with dependents living at home would experience role strain. This is not the case. Rigidities regardless of whether or not they have dependents at home are characterized by low role strain at home.[1]

On another indicator of coping style, home to work role compartmentalization, Rigidities are high, meaning that they do compartmentalize their dual roles. Another common assumption is that role compartmentalization for dual career couples without dependents is high. Relying on that assumption, one would expect the couples in this study without dependents to be high on home to work role compartmentalization. Virtually all Rigidities, regardless of whether or not dependents lived at home, did home to work role compartmentalize. Nevertheless, the indicator of dependents is useful to facilitate the discussion. The one Rigiditie couple (both in the legal profession) in this study with a dependent living at home characterize themselves as new parents and talk about being exhausted because the baby still wakes up during the night. This couple definitely compartmentalizes its roles though, and the factor that enabled this was that the wife interrupted her law career because the baby was so demanding.

> It was horrible when I went back to work after he [the baby] was born. I was nursing and the baby wouldn't take a bottle. I had to rush to the sitter's two or three times a day.... I was the first woman in the firm, and a young attorney, and they expected me to stay late and come in early (Couple 18).

Now she has just a part-time job. She can set the hours that she works, and she can complete her tasks every day. This permits her husband to spend a little quality time with her and the baby before spending the evening at his law books. For Rigidities having a dependent at home is more than just one more role obligation, it is enough of a reason to interrupt a career.

In regard to prioritizing of chores at home and prioritizing of roles, households with dependents have one more role obligation with which to deal than households without dependents. Rigidities are characterized by low prioritizing. The Rigiditie couple with a dependent gives high priority to its parent roles. As mentioned above, the wife in this couple has interrupted her law career so that she can spend more time at home with the baby and so that her husband can focus on his work knowing that she is in charge at home. Home has priority for them to such an extent that she has given up her career for the immediate future. "At home, she'll take care of everything", he says (Couple 18).

Households without dependents

Even without dependents, Rigidities have low role strain at home. Rigidities home to work role compartmentalize, and they have a high household division of labor. When they are at home they usually select their home life role over their career person role, and in this way they fulfill all of their household tasks.

Role compartmentalization means being able to separate the dual roles under consideration. This means that Rigidities do separate their roles; they keep them separate even though they do think about work occasionally when they are at home. One Rigiditie couple, both health professionals who practice medicine together, commented

> He doesn't really know I'm thinking about the office because we never discuss it at home. I usually run over the appointments for the next day every evening because I want to know what time I have to be there (Couple 21).

An occasional Rigiditie thought at home may deal with work, but Rigidities do not share the Flexie perception of the demanding nature of work and the lack of time to do it.

The hows and whats of home to work role compartmentalization are fascinating. In other words, when one is at home supposedly taking care of home life role obligations, how do thoughts of work creep in and what kind of thoughts are they? The telephone is the major way that thoughts of work creep into home life for health professionals, whether Rigiditie or Flexie. One Rigiditie couple who practice medicine together and indicate strict separation of home and work said

> Medicine does impinge on our time away from the office. One of us is on call every night and when the call is for him, I'm relieved that it's not for me (Couple 6).

Thoughts of work creep into Rigiditie households because they enjoy their work immensely and like to talk and think about it. In fact, in the whole sample, the only negative career related comment came from the Rigiditie couple, both lawyers, with a baby at home. She was not able to home to work role compartmentalize. The pressure from her job was so great that she switched to a less demanding part time job for which she really does not

51

need legal training even though the legal training helped her secure the position.

Rigidities do home to work role compartmentalize. When Rigidities are at home, they usually are not thinking about work role obligations. They are fulfilling home role obligations. The fact that Rigidities do role compartmentalize means that they are not able to fulfill their dual role obligations and this contributes to their high inter-role strain, i.e., role strain due to the competing demands of home life and careers. Since Rigidities are able to focus on home life at home, this lessens their role strain at home (intra-role strain), while at the same time increasing their inter-role strain.

Household division of labor is another indicator of coping style for Rigidities. Rigidities have a high division of household labor, meaning that they do have specific ways of accomplishing household chores.

Rigidities tend to plan who will do what chore and when, and that includes every aspect of household life including dinner preparation. Rigidities generally do not eat dinner out and do not carry in already prepared foods for dinner. That is, they plan their dinner menus ahead and whoever gets home first in the evening starts the preparation.

One Rigiditie couple (Couple 7), both academics in different departments at the same university, explained their rather unique household division of labor as follows. He, about 15 years older than her and in the transitional retirement stage, had been married for 15 years and lived alone for eight years before he met her. She had never been married before. Both, therefore, were accustomed to living alone and doing things their own way when they started living together in her house. They lived together for 10 years before getting married. They each have their own half of the house when it comes to household chores, and he contributes money for the house payment, utilities, etc. When they first began living together, they worked out a three week contract which covered all the details of home life and to see if they liked living together. She thought at first that she should do all the wife chores and he should do the husband chores, but they discovered that even though they liked living together she did not like to cook and he did not like yard work. As a result, they renegotiated parts of the contract, each takes care of his or her own part of the house, and the first one home in the evening fixes dinner.

Another rather unique system of dividing household labor comes from a two health professional Rigiditie couple (Couple 21) who have been married for 32 years and say that they each have specific sex stereotyped jobs at home except for one thing. They practice medicine together now that their children are grown up. When the children were young she did not work outside of the home. He wanted her to a "100% mother and homemaker" when the children were little. Anyhow, before she started working, he always got up early, made the coffee and brought in the newspaper. Now that she is working, he still does that, and he now goes upstairs after she gets up and makes the bed while she is having coffee and reading the newspaper. He could not do that before, he chuckles, because she was still in the bed. He goes to the office at least an hour earlier than her because she has to do her woman's work first, i.e., straighten up the kitchen and living room.

The other Rigiditie couples say that their current household division of labor is a direct result of their early years together. In one case (Couple 30), the husband was in graduate school and his wife had not yet had her graduate training. She was working full time to put him through graduate school. She was providing the income and took over running the household so he could concentrate on his studies. That is still the way they operate. Another couple (Couple 6) both of whom went to medical school at the same time and who practice medicine together said that since they were so busy with school, they made a list of what had to be done at home and who would do it. Even though the items on the list have changed, they still make the list according to their likes and dislikes. Rigiditie couples, therefore, have specific ways of ensuring the smooth operation of their households. They may change the plan from time to time or vary from it, but each person knows for which specific household role obligation they are responsible.

Related to household labor are prioritizing of chores and prioritizing of roles. Rigidities are characterized by high household division of labor and low prioritizing of chores and of roles. Since they do have a predetermined way of accomplishing household chores, Rigidities tend to ask each other for help if they find that they are having trouble completing their assigned tasks at home. Also, Rigidities do not have to make a choice between home and career roles because they role compartmentalize and work stays at the office. The interplay between dependents, household division of labor, home to work role compartmentalization, and prioritizing of chores and of roles influence the perception of role strain at home and the use of the Rigiditie style of coping.

Role strain due to the competing demands
of home life and careers

A third fact of life for Rigidities is low role strain due to the competing demands of home life and careers, i.e., inter-role strain. The indicators of coping style that are relevant here are home to work role compartmentalization, work to home role compartmentalization, and flexibility of work schedule. Rigidities are characterized by high home to work and work to home role compartmentalization and low flexibility of work schedule. These are the indicators that impact on inter-role strain.

Life for Rigidities is not circular. They role compartmentalize both at home and at work. In other words, they live two separate lives which very seldom cross. When a Rigiditie is at home, thoughts of work do not surface because Rigidities stay at work during the day and get their work done. Then, when they are at home, they can focus on nonwork related items. Likewise, when Rigidities are at work, they can concentrate fully on the demands of their work. They do not perceive their work schedule as flexible even though they are in the same professions as the Flexies. In other words, Rigidities perceive inflexible work schedules.

Rigidities, too, have learned to live with their levels of role compartmentalization and flexibility of work schedule. They have thoughts on what factors have influenced their abilities to live as dual career couples. Some factors have made their lives easier and some factors have made their lives more difficult, but none had negative feelings about the dual career lifestyle.

Factors which have made the lifestyle more difficult for Rigidities vary. "Nothing makes it hard", says a Rigiditie couple who are both academics in different departments at the same university (Couple 7). The demands of the profession are rigorous, but they knew that when they started their careers. "Always being on call makes it hard", says another Rigiditie couple (Couple 6) who practice medicine together. "Making sure that our family gets a reasonable share of time and that the kids don't get gypped", makes the lifestyle difficult for another Rigiditie couple, one an academic and the other a health professional (Couple 30). The one Rigiditie couple with a dependent at home (Couple 18), both in the legal profession, say what makes it hard for them is

> A child -- without a child we would have money, and she could have any job she wanted and not be tired. Without a child, she could commute and not worry about working late. Having a child prohibits all that because of the responsibility you have to the child.

Another Rigiditie couple who practice medicine together (Couple 21) say that each having strong personalities makes it difficult for them. They argued over how late the office should be open at night, and they compromised. He stays there until 9 p.m., and she goes home at 5 p.m. Rigidities note a variety of factors which make the dual career lifestyle hard.

They also note the factors which make the lifestyle easy. Cooperation, understanding, and enjoyment of the profession are what makes it easy for Rigidities. "The understanding of each other's responsibilities at work" (Couple 21) and "both having the same sense of dedication and recognizing the importance work plays" (Couple 7) are the factors which help these couples live as Rigiditie dual career couples. "It's the whole family cooperating and working together", says Couple 30, "that enables us to survive". Other Rigidities say it is easy because it is what they want to do.

We like being doctors! Medicine is exciting, even though some cases are puzzling. The interaction of family life and medicine, that is, for example, helping family members deal with a terminally ill family member is what makes medicine exciting (Couple 6).

Rigidities, therefore, think that there are some factors which facilitate the dual career lifestyle and some factors that make it difficult.

Notes

1 Only one Rigiditie couple had a dependent living at home. In contrast, 17 Flexie couples had dependents living at home.

6 What it all means

Dual career couples cope with the role strain caused by the competing demands of their home life and careers using either a Flexible coping style or a Rigid coping style. This chapter summarizes the Flexie and the Rigiditie styles of coping with role strain, offers conclusions of the research, and discusses implications for future research and policy.

Summary

All research is characterized by hypotheses, and the basic hypotheses at the beginning of this study were that role strain exists for dual career couples and that different couple styles of coping with role strain exist. Based on this, the Flexie and Rigiditie styles of coping with role strain were elaborately and conceptually defined using the indicators of coping style.

Indicators of couple coping style were role compartmentalization, schedule flexibility, household division of labor, prioritizing, and dependents. Role compartmentalization had two dimensions, and Flexies and Rigidities were different on these dimensions. Low role compartmentalization was a Flexie characteristic while Rigidities were characterized by high role compartmentalization. In other words, Flexies do not separate their dual roles, and Rigidities do.

Schedule flexibility also had two dimensions, and Flexies and Rigidities were significantly different on these two dimensions. Flexies were characterized by high schedule flexibility, and low schedule flexibility characterized Rigidities. In other words, Flexies felt they could leave work whenever they wanted to, and Rigidities felt they could not leave work.

Flexies and Rigidities also differed in regard to household division of labor. Flexies were characterized by low household division of labor while Rigidities were characterized by high household division of labor. Flexies were reactive to household responsibilities, doing something only when it had to be done. Rigidities were proactive. That is they developed schedules and other ways of keeping the household running smoothly so that they did not have to react to emergencies.

Flexies and Rigidities differed in their prioritizing of chores at home and roles. Flexies were characterized by high prioritizing, meaning that they tended to ignore chores at home and that if they were at home they usually selected their home life role over their career person role when a choice was necessary. Rigidities, on the other hand, were characterized by low prioritizing, meaning that they tended to accomplish all chores at home and that they usually selected the role which they were playing at the time the choice was necessary.

The final indicator was having dependents at home. Surprisingly, this was not a significant indicator of role strain for either Flexies or for Rigidities.

Therefore, according to this research, there are two distinct coping styles which dual career couples use to manage their role strain. Flexies and Rigidities both have role strain at work, role strain at home, and role strain due to the competing demands of home life and work. However, they have different levels of these role strains. Flexies have high role strain at work, high role strain at home, and low role strain due to the competing demands of home life and work. Rigidities, on the other hand, have low role strain at work, low role strain at home, and high role strain due to the competing demands of home life and careers.

The key indicators of the two coping styles are flexibility of work schedule, home to work role compartmentalization, and work to home role compartmentalization. In other words, Flexies have high role strain at work because they have flexible jobs. They leave work during the day to take care of nonwork related obligations, and as a result do not get everything done at work. Flexies also have high role strain at home because they have low household division of labor. They ignore things at home in order to take care of work related chores. However, Flexies have low role strain due to the competing demands of home life and careers and low home to work and work to home role compartmentalization. Since they can leave work during the day for nonwork related reasons and since they can finish their work at home in the evenings or on weekends, they do not feel much difficulty fulfilling the obligations of either role.

Rigidities, on the other hand, have low role strain at work because their jobs are not flexible. They cannot leave work, so they do not even think about it. Rigidities also have low role strain at home. They have a high household division of labor which means that chores do not get ignored but get completed in a timely fashion because they are scheduled in advance. However, Rigidities have high role strain due to the competing demands of home life and careers and high role compartmentalization. They feel difficulty in fulfilling the obligations of their dual roles. However, since they are very role compartmentalized, they do not think about home at work or about work at home. These are the main indicators that affect whether a couple uses a flexible or a rigid coping style.

Conclusions

Theoretical and methodological

This book is a major theoretical and methodological contribution to the dual career couple literature because it conceptualizes a way of collecting and analyzing couple data to discern how couples cope with role strain. In doing this, the book clarifies and defines the concept of dual career couple coping style by operationalizing and analyzing the concepts of role strain, role compartmentalization, household division of labor, flexibility of work schedule, dependents, and prioritizing.

The typology has two cells -- Flexies and Rigidities. These are, in the Weberian (1949, pp. 89-94) sense, ideal types. They are ideal types of dual career couple styles of coping with role strain. The ideal type Flexie is characterized by high role strain at home, high role strain at work, high flexibility of work schedule, high prioritizing of chores and roles, and low role strain due to the competing demands of home life and careers, low role compartmentalization, and low household division of labor. The ideal type Rigiditie is characterized by low role strain at home, low role strain at work, low flexibility of work schedule, low prioritizing of chores and roles, and high role strain due to the competing demands of home life and careers, high role compartmentalization, and high household division of labor. The indicators of coping style are the same for each coping style, but the measure of the indicator differs for each coping style. That is, for example, both Flexies and Rigidities have role strain at home, but it is high for Flexies and low for Rigidities.

This typology of dual career couple coping styles fills a theoretical gap in the scholarly dual career couple literature. Previous dual career couple research literature has documented quite extensively the fact that role strain does exist in the dual career couple and that couple members, particularly wives, have had to cope with the role strain. Some of the techniques that couple members have used to cope with their role strain have been identified, but have not been dealt with conceptually. The previous research, like this research, has been descriptive and narrative in form and analysis. However, this book does more than just summarize what wives or husbands said separately in response to items on a questionnaire. Joint husband wife interviews yielded the data used for delineating these coping styles.

There are major theoretical and methodological conclusions. First, alternative dual career couple styles of coping with role strain exist. These alternative coping styles are the Flexie coping style and the Rigiditie coping styles.

Second, a method now exists for determining how dual career couples cope with the competing demands of their home life and careers exists. This method could be utilized by other researchers of dual career couples in various ways. For example, Rapoport and Rapoport (1969), Hall and Hall (1979), and Holahan and Gilbert (1979) could reevaluate their dual career couple research in light of these conclusions to see if the Flexie Rigiditie typology could be imposed on their samples. Future researchers could also utilize these conclusions to see if the typology could be replicated.

Significance for therapy, research
and policy

The more practical conclusions have to do with how the theoretical and methodological conclusions can be applied to the everyday life of dual career couples in order to alleviate some of the role strain that exists for them. Dual career couples can decide based on the ideal type characteristics, either by themselves or with the help of a counselor, whether they use the Flexie or the Rigiditie coping style. Once they know, they can either learn how to live with the style they use or try to change. Since the indicators are very clearly defined, they can attack the indicator with which they are not satisfied. For example, suppose the dual career couple discovers they use the Flexie coping style and that their inability to role compartmentalize either at home or at work is causing them a great deal of role strain that they would like to ease. They can make a direct attempt to compartmentalize their roles. That is, they can decide that, like a Rigiditie couple, they will only leave work during the day for an extreme emergency. In that way they would complete their daily obligations at work, not bring work home, and be able to spend time with their families or friends in the evening without worrying about a work task that must be completed for the next day. In other words, the Flexie Rigiditie typology and the indicators of each can be used by dual career couples to manage their everyday lives. They can come to understand that the role strain they experience is not unique to them, but is a common occurrence in modern industrial society. This realization can encourage coping styles.

There is also significance related to the changing roles of women and men. Neither men nor women are stuck in their traditional gender stereotyped roles because as is shown in this book not only can women pursue careers but men can also take care of household chores and dependents.

There is a vast territory of the dual career couple lifestyle that has not been touched. This book, for the most part, was limited in scope to successful dual career couples living in one locale who agreed to participate in the research. Those dual career couples who are separated geographically because their jobs are in different geographical locations may have their own unique situations with which to cope.

This book was also limited to couples in only three professions. There are many other professions which exist, and future research could investigate some of them. In addition, there are many dual earner couples, i.e., those couples not pursuing professions, but just plain working at jobs. Those couples who are in low flexibility jobs probably experience the same role strains that dual career couples face. A possible definition of a dual earner couple could paraphrase the definition of a dual career couple. That is, a dual earner couple is a husband and wife who both work at jobs and maintain a family life together which may or may not include dependents and who live without a "wife". Do these dual earner couples fit into the flexible rigid typology, or do they have their own coping styles? Some of the other avenues that future research could investigate include the possibility that the same indicators of coping style exist for dual earner couples as exist for dual career couples and that other indicators of coping style exist for both dual earner and dual career couples, as well as how these possible other indicators fit into the Flexie Rigiditie typology.

Future research on dual career couples, particularly the flexible rigid typology, could address other factors which were not addressed in this book. A large national probability sample would enable future research to address many more factors associated with the dual career or dual earner lifestyle. This might show that there are other types of coping styles such as switchers, avoiders, and noninteractors which should be looked for and examined. In that way future studies on the dual career couple could have a larger and more professionally mixed sample.

There would be advantages to a larger sample. If a national, or even regional, sample of randomly selected dual career couples could be interviewed or be subjected to a mail questionnaire, then there would be much more data with which to work. If the sample were large enough, then the assumptions of levels of measurement higher than nominal level could be honored and statistical tests could be employed in the analysis. In this way a determination regarding the Flexie Rigiditie typology could be made with a level of confidence. Using these more advanced levels of measurement, Flexies and Rigidities could be more precisely measured and placed on a continuum.

Another advantage to a larger sample which meets the assumptions regarding the higher levels of measurement would be that other sources of role strain beyond the realm of this book could be measured. One of these other sources of role strain is work load variance. For example, even though persons are pursuing the same profession, their work loads may be different. That is, just because two persons are both criminal lawyers does not mean that they work the same number of hours. One may have more office staff and clerks who do the preliminary research which the lawyer requires, or one may limit his/her number of cases for the express reason of wanting to be more of a family person. Another source of role strain for a dual career couple could be geographical separation due to having jobs in different geographic locations, having a job that requires a lot of extended travel, or one of the spouses in the couple receiving a job promotion contingent on relocating.

Dual career families include people other than the husband and wife. They include dependents. How do dependents, especially children, feel about both of their parents working? Children exist in all age groups. What is the affect on children of different ages of having parents both of whom work? Parents whose children are at day care five full days a week like to say that their preschool age children are developing self reliance and becoming independent individuals. These parents do not like to say that they are neglecting their children. How the children actually feel could be the subject of future research. Parents of children who care for themselves before and after school until the parents arrive home from work like to say that their children are learning responsibility in addition to self reliance and independence. These parents do not like to think that their children could be scared to enter the house alone or that their children could be engaging in some activity of which the parents do not approve. Future research could address how the children actually feel about their self care situation. Future research could also study college age children of dual career couples to determine how these older children feel about coming home to visit over their school holidays and finding that their parents must go away on a business trip or have a project they must finish. How do children of dual career couples cope with their feelings? Presumably there would be alternative child styles of coping with feelings, and future research could develop a typology of these alternative styles measuring a variety of indicators of feelings. Future research could play a major role in showing children that their situation is not unique to them and thereby encourage coping styles.

All of these suggestions for future research indicate the significance that this book has for family policy development. Family policy is social policy that takes into account the impact that a policy will have on families (Stanfield, 1992; Zimmerman, 1988). All families need governmental services to attain a sense of family well being, and therefore it is important to think about policy in relation to all families. Family policy introduces a family perspective into the policy arena. All families, not just those in dual career marriages, could benefit from policy that used a family perspective (Zimmerman 1988). Using a family perspective means that policymakers would incorporate family criteria into policy (Golonka and Hutchins, 1992). For example, when providing services to individuals, policies and programs must consider families as partners to the individual and policies and programs must recognize the diversity of family life. Also, policies should encourage and reinforce family commitment and stability and should support and supplement family functioning.

When Goode's (1960) theory of role strain is combined, for example, with Hill's ABCX theory of family crisis management (Hill, 1958), then a family stress perspective exists which can help in the development of family policy. As Zimmerman (1988) says, policy developed from the perspective of family stress theory would attempt to increase the resources available to families and to reduce the demands on families so that they could maintain their equilibrium. Simply put, policy developed with a family stress perspective could lessen the role strain that is normal in modern industrial society.

APPENDIX A

APPENDIX A

Interview schedule: coping

Couple #: _____

Couple Type: <u>VAR001</u>

Introduction: My study is about married people who work and the relationship between their home lives and work lives. I have asked you to participate because you are a married couple and you both work. The first questions deal with your home life.

VAR002　1.　When you are at home, do you ever think about work; for example plan tomorrow's work activities, reflect on the work day, or plan long-range work activities?

(IF BOTH SAY NO, GO TO #4)　　　　<u>Husband</u>　<u>Wife</u>

yes _____

no _____

VAR003　2.　Why is that?

VAR004　3.　How does the fact that you think about work at home affect your relationship? (probe on: perceptions and actions)

VAR005　4.　When you are at home, do you feel like you have enough time there to do everything you want to do?

(IF BOTH SAY YES, GO TO #10)　　　　<u>Husband</u>　<u>Wife</u>

yes _____

no _____

VAR006   5.   When you have more things to do at home than you have time for, do you usually ignore certain things or ask other for help?

	Husband	Wife
ignore		
ask others		

VAR007   6.   Why is that?

VAR008   7.   How do you decide which to do?

VAR009   8.   What kinds of things might you consider doing if you had more time at home?

VAR010   9.   Could you give me an example of a time you decided to do one thing instead of another? (probe: what do you mean, why)

VAR011   10.   Do you have someone living at home who is dependent on you like a young child would be?
(IF NO DEPENDENT, GO TO #20)

	yes	no

VAR012   11.   Can either of you do as much as you'd like to with them?

	Husband	Wife
yes		
no		

VAR013   12.   Can either of you take them to routine or emergency health care appointments during your work day?

	Husband	Wife
yes		
no		

VAR014   13.   Can either of you take them other places, like movies or out to lunch during your work day?

	Husband	Wife
yes		
no		

VAR015   14.   How do you work out who does these things?

VAR016　15.　How do you arrange the time to do these things?

VAR017　16.　Why do you think you do (or don't do) as much with
VAR018　　them as you'd like to?

VAR019　17.　How does having a dependent affect you, both at
VAR020　　home and the office?

VAR021　18.　How would you like to do more/less with them?
VAR022

VAR023　19.　How does the amount of time you spend with your
　　dependent(s) affect your relationship?　(probe on:
　　perceptions and actions)

I have a few more questions about your home life and household activities.

VAR024　20.　Do you hire outside help for such things as
　　housecleaning, yard work, cooking, or laundry?

　　　　　　　yes　no
　　　　　　　_____

VAR025　21.　How many times a week do you usually eat out? ___

VAR026　22.　How many times a week do you usually carry in
　　already prepared food for dinner? _____

VAR027　23.　Could you give me an example of a chore that you
　　hire out?

VAR028　24.　In regard to household chores, I have a series of
VAR029　　items and I'd like you to tell me who does what? (x
　　indicates who does it)

Other

		Husband	Wife	Internal	External
a.	vacuuming				
b.	dusting				
c.	laundry				
d.	daily trash				
e.	weekly trash				
f.	make beds				
g.	clean toilet				

h.	clean bathtub	_____
i.	mow and water lawn	_____
j.	plan meals	_____
k.	clean up dishes	_____
l.	grocery shopping	_____
m.	car maintenance	_____
n.	make social plans	_____
o.	arrange sitters	_____
p.	pay bills	_____
q.	financial planning	_____
r.	take care of pet	_____

VAR030   25.   Why do you divide the chores up this way?

VAR031   26.   How did you decide on this way of doing it?

VAR032   27.   How would you say it's working out?

VAR033   28.   Could you give me an example of how you share a specific chore?

VAR034   29.   Now I'd like to ask a few questions about your jobs. (x means yes)

		Husband	Wife
a.	Do you have regular set hours?		_____
b.	Can you avoid rush hour traffic?		_____
c.	Can you go in a little later or leave a little earlier than usual?		_____
d.	Can you leave to go to health care appointments?		_____
e.	Can you go on personal errands		_____
f.	Can you go shopping?		_____
g.	Can you leave to do things like drop your pet off to be groomed or do your banking business?		_____

68

VAR035   30.   Do you feel like you have enough time at work to do everything you want to do there?

	Husband	Wife
Yes		
no		

VAR036   31.   When you are at work, do you ever think about home; for example plan tomorrow's home activities, reflect on the day at home, or plan long-range home activities?

(IF BOTH SAY NO, GO TO #35)

	Husband	Wife
yes		
no		

VAR037   32.   Why do you take the time during the day to think
VAR038   about or do these kinds of things?

VAR039   33.   How are you able to do this?

VAR040   34.   Could you give me an example of the kind of thing
VAR041   you might think about or take time during the day to do?

Now I'd like to ask a few questions about the way work and home affect each other.

VAR042   35.   When you have to do something at the office at the same time you have to be at home, do you usually do the thing at the office or the thing at home?

	Husband	Wife
office		
home		

VAR043   36.   Why do you choose one over the other?

VAR044   37.   How are you able to do it?

VAR045   38.   Could you give me an example of a time you decided in favor of either home
VAR046   office?

VAR047   39.   Do you feel like you spend too much time at the office to do everything you want to do at home?

Husband   Wife

yes   _____

no   _____

VAR048   40.   Do you feel like you spend too much time at home to do everything you want to do at the office?

Husband   Wife

yes   _____

no   _____

VAR049
VAR050   41.   You've told me a lot about how it is being married people who work. Think back over the kinds of things we've been talking about, and tell me what the most important factor that makes the situation easy or hard to deal with is.

THANK YOU VERY MUCH FOR SPENDING THIS TIME WITH ME.

APPENDIX B

APPENDIX B

Measures, methods of analysis, and the sample

Measures

Role strain, role compartmentalization, division of household labor, flexibility of work schedule, prioritizing, and dependents were the indicators of coping style. Each was operationalized through one or more questions on the interview schedule (see Appendix A) in the following way.

Role strain

Role strain was defined conceptually as the felt difficulty in fulfilling role demands. There were three dimensions to role strain. One was role strain at home, or felt difficulty in fulfilling role demands at home. This was operationalized in question number 4:

> When you are at home, do you feel like you have enough time there to do everything you want to do?

Respondents could score high or low on this question. A high score indicated high role strain, and a low score indicated low role strain. If both husband and wife answered "yes" to the question, the response was coded as "1". If one said "yes" and one said "no" to the question, the response was coded "2". If both said "no" to the question, the response was coded as "3". A score of "1" or "2" was interpreted as low, while a score of "3" was interpreted as high. A second dimension was role strain at work, or felt difficulty in fulfilling role demands at work. This was operationalized in question number 30:

73

Do you feel like you have enough time at work to do everything you want to do there?

Respondents could score high or low on this question. A high score indicated high role strain, and a low score indicated low role strain. If both husband and wife answered "yes" to the question, the response was coded as "1". If one said "yes" and one said "no" to the question, the responses was coded as "2". If both said "no" to the question, the response was coded as "3". A score of "1" or "2" was interpreted as low, while a score of "3" was interpreted as high. A third dimension of role strain was the felt difficulty in fulfilling the competing demands of home life and careers. This was operationalized in question numbers 39 and 40:

Do you feel like you spend too much time at the office to do everything you want to do at home?

Do you feel like you spend too much time at home to do everything you want to do at the office?

Respondents could score high or low on these questions. A high score indicated high role strain, and a low score indicated low role strain. If both husband and wife answered "no" to these questions, the responses were coded as "1". If one said "yes" and one said "no", the responses were coded as "2". If both said "yes" to these questions, the responses were coded as "3". A score of "1" or "2" was interpreted as low, while a score of "3" was interpreted as high.

Role compartmentalization

Role compartmentalization was defined conceptually as the ability to separate roles distinctly. There were two dimensions to role compartmentalization. One dimension was being at home and thinking about work. This was operationalized in question numbers 1 and 2:

When you are at home, do you ever think about work; for example plan tomorrow's work activities, reflect on the work day, or plan long-range work activities?

Why is that?

Respondents could score high or low on question number 1. A high score indicated high role compartmentalization, and a low score indicated low role compartmentalization. If both husband and wife answered "yes" to the

74

question, the response was coded as "1". If one said "no" and one said "yes," the response was coded as "2." If both said "no" to the question, the response was coded as "3". A score of "1" or "2" was interpreted as low, while a score of "3" was interpreted as high. Question number 2 was an open-ended question, and was not scored.

The other dimension of role compartmentalization was being at work and thinking about home. This was operationalized in question numbers 31, 32, 33, and 34.

> When you are at work, do you ever think about home; for example plan tomorrow's home activities, reflect on the day at home, or plan long-range home activities?

> Why do you take the time during the day to think about these kinds of things?

> How are you able to do this?

> Could you give me an example of the kind of thing you might think about or take time during the day to do?

Respondents could score high or low on question number 31. A high score indicated high role compartmentalization and a low score indicated low role compartmentalization If both husband and wife answered "yes" to the question, the response was coded as "1". If one said "yes" and one said "no", the response was coded as "2". If both said "no", the response was coded as "3". A score of "1" or "2" was interpreted as low, while a score of "3" was interpreted as high. Question numbers 32, 33, and 34 were open-ended and were not scored.

Division of household labor

Division of household labor was defined conceptually as the couple's arrangement of who does what to keep the household running smoothly. There were two dimensions to division of household labor. One dimension referred to using people or services external to the family to help keep the household running smoothly. This was operationalized in question numbers 20, 21, 22, and 23.

> Do you hire outside help for such things as housecleaning, yard work, cooking, or laundry?

> How many times a week do you usually eat dinner out?

How many times a week do you usually carry in already prepared food for dinner?

Could you give me an example of a chore that you hire out?

Respondents answered either "yes" or "no" to question number 20. Questions numbers 21 and 22 required the respondent to give a "number of times". Answers could range from 0 to 7 times a week. Question number 23 was an open-ended question and was not scored. The other dimension of division of labor referred to what the family members did to keep the household running smoothly. This was operationalized in question numbers 24, 25, 26, 27, and 28.

In regard to household chores, I have a series of items and I'd like you to tell me who does what.
a. vacuuming
b. dusting
c. laundry
d. daily trash
e. weekly trash
f. make beds
g. clean toilet
h. clean bathtub
i. mow and water lawn
j. plan meals
k. clean up dishes
l. grocery shopping
m. car maintenance
n. make social plans
o. arrange sitters
p. pay bills
q. financial planning
r. take care of pet

Why do you divide the chores up this way?

How did you decide on this way of doing it?

How would you say it's working out?

Could you give me an example of how you share a specific chore?

Question number 24 was scored two ways. One way measured degree of internalness, and respondents could score high or low. A high score indicated a high degree of internalness, and a low score indicated a low degree of internalness. If the respondents received checks in 25 or less of the boxes, the response was coded and scored as low. If they received checks in 26 or more of the boxes, the response was coded and scored as high.

The other way measured internal division of labor. Respondents could score high or low. A high score indicated a high household division of labor, and a low score indicated a low household division of labor. If the chore was hired out, ignored, or not applicable to the couple, the response was coded as "0". If one person in the household did the chore, the response was coded as "1". If two people did the chore, the response was coded as "2". If three or more people in the household did the chore, the response was coded as "3". A score of "1" was interpreted as low, and a score of "2" or "3" was interpreted as high. Question numbers 25, 26, 27, and 28 were open-ended and were not scored.

Flexibility of work schedule

Flexibility of work schedule was defined conceptually as a schedule that permits a person to leave work for a nonwork related reason. There were two dimension of work flexibility. One dimension was flexibility in regard to dependents. This was operationalized in question numbers 12 and 13:

Can either of you take them to routine or emergency health care appointments during your work day?

Can either of you take them other places, like movies or out to lunch, during your work day?

Respondents could score high or low on question numbers 12 and 13. A high score indicated a high degree of flexibility in regard to dependents. If both husband and wife answered "no" to the questions, the response was coded as "1". If one said "yes" and one said "no", the response was coded as "2". If both said "yes", the response was coded as "3". A score of "1" or "2" was interpreted as low, and a score of "3" was interpreted as high. The other dimension of flexibility of work schedule referred to the actual flexibility of the work schedule. This was operationalized in question number 29:

Now I'd like to ask a few questions about your jobs.
a.   Do you have regular set hours?

b.   Can you avoid rush hour traffic?

c.   Can you go in a little later or leave a little earlier than usual?

d.   Can you leave to go to health care appointments?

e.   Can you go on personal errands?

f.   Can you go shopping?

g.   Can you leave to do things like drop your pet off to be groomed or do your banking business?

Respondents could score either high or low on this question. A high score indicated a high degree of work flexibility, and a low score indicated a low degree of work flexibility. If the respondents received check marks in 10 or less of the boxes, the response was coded and scored as low. If they received check marks in 11 or more of the boxes, the response was coded and scored as high.

Prioritizing

Prioritizing was defined conceptually as a couple deciding that one thing or role was more important than another. There were two dimension of prioritizing. One dimension had to do with chores at home. This was operationalized in question numbers 5, 6, 7, 8, and 9:

When you have more things to do at home than you have time for, do you usually ignore certain things or ask others for help?

Why is that?

How do you decide which to do?

What kinds of things might you consider doing if you have more time at home?

Could you give me an example of a time you decided to do one thing instead of another?

Respondents could score either high or low on question number 5. A high score indicated high prioritizing of chores at home, and a low score indicated low prioritizing of chores at home. If either the husband or the wife ignored chores and the other one asked for help, the response was coded as "1". If both asked for help, the response was coded as "2". If both ignored, the response was coded as "3". A score of "1" or "2" was interpreted as low, and a score of "3" was interpreted as high. Question numbers 6, 7, 8, and 9 were open-ended and were not scored. The other dimension of prioritizing referred to home versus work roles. This was operationalized in question numbers 35, 36, 37, and 38:

> When you have to do something at the office at the same time you have to be at home, do you usually do the thing at the office or the thing at home?

> Why do you choose one over the other?

> How are you able to do it?

> Could you give me an example of a time you decided in favor of either home or office?

Respondents could score either high or low on question number 35. A high score indicated high prioritizing of roles, and a low score indicated low prioritizing of roles. If either the husband or the wife did office and the other did home, the response was coded as "1". If both do the home thing, the response was coded as "2". If both said they do the office thing, the response was coded as "3". A score of "1" or "2" was interpreted as low and a score of "3" was interpreted as high. Question numbers 36, 37, and 38 were open-ended and were not scored.

Dependents

Dependents was defined conceptually as someone living at home who would be dependent on the parents like a young child would be. Dependents could be young children, chronically ill persons, or elderly parents living at home. There were five dimensions to dependents. The first dimension dealt with the presence or absence of a dependent. This was operationalized in question number 10:

> Do you have someone living at home who is dependent on you like a young child would be?

Respondents answered either "yes" or "no" to this question. The second dimension referred to time spent with dependents. This was operationalized in question numbers 11, 15, 16, and 18:

> Can either of you do as much as you'd like to with them?

> How do you arrange the time to do these things?

Why do you think you do (or don't do) as much with them as you'd like to?

How would you like to do more/less with them?

Respondents could score either high or low on question number 11. If both husband and wife said "no" to the question, the response was coded as "1". If one said "yes" and one said "no", the response was coded as "2". If both said "yes", the response was coded as "3". A score of "1" or "2" was interpreted as low, and a score of "3" was interpreted as high. Question numbers 15, 16, and 18 were open-ended and were not scored. The third dimension of dependents referred to who dealt with the dependent(s). This was operationalized in question number 14:

How do you work out who does these things?

This was an open-ended question. The fourth dimension of dependents referred to the impacts of dependents. This was operationalized in question number 17:

How does having a dependent affect you, both at home and the office?

This was an open-ended question. The fifth dimension of dependents referred to spousal relations in light of the time spent with dependents. This was operationalized in question number 19:

How does the amount of time you spend with your dependent(s) affect your relationship?

This was an open-ended question.

Method of analysis

Data analysis was done both quantitatively and qualitatively. Quantitative analysis has assumptions regarding the level of measurement used in data collection (Bailey, 1978). Then, depending on the level of measurement used in data collection, statistical analysis can be used to test the significance of results or reliability (Robinson, 1957) in order to determine the meaning of the data.

The level of measurement used in this study was nominal level data, i.e., categorical data. This level of measurement permits categorical quantitative analysis. Data were collected, coded and tabulated as explained above in the

Measures section. At this point, the alternative dual career couple styles of coping with role strain were determined. Cross-classification tables were constructed for each indicator of coping style. Coping style was at the top of the table and the indicator of coping style was on the left hand side of the table. The cells formed by the juxtaposition of the coping styles with the indicators of coping style were filled with descriptive percentages and actual numbers of couples in each coping style. In this way, each of the alternative couple styles of coping with role strain was described in relation to the specific indicator.

Analysis was also done qualitatively. The research steps leading up to qualitative analysis are just as rigorous as the ones leading up to quantitative analysis (Schwartz and Jacobs, 1979) even though the assumptions regarding level of measurement are less stringent.

There are different ways of doing qualitative analysis such as content analysis and interpreting life histories (Schwartz and Jacobs, 1979). Another way of doing qualitative analysis is to actually combine quantitative with qualitative analysis. In other words, as done in this study, nominal level or categorical data (Black and Champion, 1976) can be used to approximate numerical values and give, e.g., high low or agree disagree, scores to the data. Then these categorical scores along with respondents' life histories or responses to probe questions can be used to develop the qualitative analysis.

The qualitative analysis for this research was done in the following manner. The concept of role strain was multidimensional, i.e., role strain at work, role strain at home, and role strain due to the competing demands of home life and careers. These dimensions of role strain were the organizing factors along which Flexies and Rigidities were described. The description included how each relevant indicator of coping style related to the coping style utilized. For example, the indicators of work to home role compartmentalization, schedule flexibility, dependents, and prioritizing of roles were the indicators which related to role strain at work. The indicators of household division of labor, home to work role compartmentalization, dependents, prioritizing of chores at home, and prioritizing of roles related to role strain at home. Home to work role compartmentalization, work to home role compartmentalization, and flexibility of work schedule were the indicators that related to role strain due to the competing demands of home life and careers.

The qualitative analysis filled in the framework of the Flexie and Rigiditie coping styles which the quantitative analysis defined. This expansion and elaboration of the quantitative framework was accomplished by weaving in the couple respondents' responses to the open-ended questions. In other words, in addition to the narrative description of the concepts and indicators, actual quotes of couple respondents were incorporated into the analysis in order to more clearly define the Flexie and Rigiditie coping styles.

81

This study like other studies in the social sciences involved decision-making. As Campbell and Katona (1953) said in regard to exploratory field studies, these decisions have to do with the precision of observations and generalizeability, i.e., measurement, method of analysis, and generalizing beyond the sample to the population.

During the process of the study, decisions were made regarding the type of data collected. Data was collected through personal interviews, and open-ended questions outnumbered forced-choice questions because the purpose of the research was to typologize and to describe how the dual career couple copes with the competing demands of home life and careers. In other words, the best way to find out how they cope, is to ask and let them explain. Therefore, data were qualitative.

The decision was also made to limit the sample to 36 dual career couples. The purpose of the research, theoretical saturation and depth of data were achieved with this sample size. This relatively small sample size discourages the use of low level statistical tests of significance. Therefore, any conclusions can only be applied to this sample. However, the same instrument and procedures could be used in further research to see if the conclusions hold. This is a goal of scientific research: i.e., replication of studies.

The sample

A total of 82 dual career couples were contacted through snowball sampling. However, 46 chose not to participate, and so the sample consisted of 36 dual career couples.

The 36 dual career couples were contacted and interviewed during the seven-week period from April 24, 1986, to June 5, 1986. Of these 36 couples, 25 of the couples were pursuing the same profession. That is, 25 of the couples were either both pursuing careers in the health profession, the legal profession, or the academic profession. The remaining 11 couples were pursuing different careers, but the only permissible careers were in the health profession, the legal profession, and the academic profession.

Bibliography

Aldous, Joan (1981), "From Dual-Earner to Dual Career and Back Again", *Journal of Family Issues*, Vol. 2, pp. 115-25.

Angell, Robert C. (1936), *The Family Encounters the Depression*, Charles Scribners' Sons: New York.

Bailey, Kenneth D. (1978), *Methods of Social Research*, Free Press: New York.

Berman, E., Sacks, S. and Lief, H. (1975), "The Two-professional Marriage: A New Conflict Syndrome", *Journal of Sex and Marital Therapy*, Vol. 1, pp. 242-53.

Bingham, Walter Van Dyke, Moore, Bruce and Gustad, John W. (1959), *How to Interview*, Harper & Row: New York.

Black, James A. and Champion, Dean J. (1976), *Methods and Issues in Social Research*, John Wiley and Sons: New York.

Blalock, Hubert M., Jr (1972), *Social Statistics*, McGraw Hill: New York.

Bryson, R., Bryson, J. and Johnson, M. (1978), "Family Size, Satisfaction, and Productivity in Dual-career Couples", *Psychology of Women Quarterly*, Vol. 3, pp. 67-77.

Burgess, Ernest W. (1926), "The Family as a Unity of Interacting Personalities", *Family*, Vol. 7, pp. 3-9.

Burr, Wesley R. (1973), *Theory Construction and the Sociology of the Family*, John Wiley & Sons: London.

Campbell, D.T., Angus, A. and Katona, George (1953), "The Sample Survey: A Technique for Social Science Research", in Festinger, Leon and Katz, Daniel (eds.), *Research Methods in the Behavioral Sciences*, Dryden Press: New York.

Campbell, Donald T. and Stanley, Julian C. (1968), *Experimental and Quasi-Experimental Design for Research*, Rand McNally: Chicago.

Carmines, Edward and Zeller, Richard (1979), *Reliability and Validity Assessment*, Sage: Beverly Hills.

Cavan, R.S. and Ranck, K.H. (1938), *The Family and the Depression*, University of Chicago Press: Chicago.

Christiansen, Harold (1964), *Handbook of Marriage and the Family*, Rand McNally: Chicago.

Cleveland, Martha Elmquist (1977), "Family Adaptation to the Permanent Disablement of a Son or Daughter", unpublished doctoral dissertation, University of Minnesota:Minneapolis.

Cooley, Charles H. (1902), *Human Nature and the Social Order*, Charles Scribner's Sons: New York.

Cuber, John and Haroff, Peggy (1968), *The Significant Americans*, Penguin: Baltimore.

Epstein, Cynthia F. (1971), "Law Partners and Marital Partners: Strains and Solutions in the Dual-career Family Enterprise", *Human Relations*, Vol. 24, pp. 549-64.

Getzels, J.W. and Guba, E.G. (1954), "Role, Role Conflict, and Effectiveness: An Empirical Study", *American Sociological Review*, Vol. 19, pp. 164-75.

Gilbert, L.A., Holahan, C.K. and Manning, L. (1981), "Coping with Conflict Between Professional and Maternal Roles", *Family Relations*, Vol. 30, pp. 419-26.

Gilliland, N.C. (1979), "The Problem of Geographic Mobility for Dual Career Families", *Journal of Comparative Family Studies*, Vol. 10, pp. 345-58.

Glaser, Bernard G. and Strauss, Anselm L. (1967), *The Discovery of Grounded Theory*, Aldine Publishing: Chicago.

Goffman, Erving (1961), *Asylums: Essays on the Social Situation of Mental Patients and Other Inmates*, Anchor/Doubleday: New York.

Golonka, Susan and Hutchins, John, (1992), *COFO Family Policy Report*, Vol.2, No. 1, Consortium of Family Organizations: Washington, D.C.

Goode, William J. (1960), "A Theory of Role Strain", *American Sociological Review*, Vol. 25, pp. 483-96.

Goode, William (1963), *World Revolution and Family Patterns*, The Free Press: New York.

Goode, William (1964), *The Family*, Prentice-Hall, Inc: Englewood Cliffs, NJ.

Gorden, Raymond L. (1975), *Interviewing: Strategy, Techniques, and Tactics*, The Dorsey Press: Homewood, IL.

Goyer, Robert S., Redding, W. Charles and Rickey, John T. (1968), *Interviewing Principles and Techniques: A Project Text*, William C. Brown: Dubuque, IA.

Gross, H.E. (1980), "Dual Career Couples Who Live Apart: Two Types",

Journal of Marriage and the Family, Vol. 42, pp. 567-77.

Hall, D.T. (1972), "A Model of Coping with Role Conflict: The Role Behavior of College Educated Women", *Administrative Science Quarterly*, Vol. 17, pp. 471-86.

Hall, Francine S. and Hall, Douglas T. (1979), *The Two-Career Couple*, Addison-Wesley: Menlo Park, CA.

Handel, Warren (1979), "Normative Expectations and the Emergence of Meaning as Solutions to Problems: Convergence of Structural and Interactionist Views", *American Journal of Sociology*, Vol. 84, pp. 855-81.

Hansen, Donald and Hill, Reuben (1964), "Families Under Stress", in Christiansen, Harold (ed.), *Handbook of Marriage and the Family*, Rand McNally: Chicago, pp. 782-819.

Heckman, N.A., Bryson, B. and Bryson, J. (1977), "Problems of Professional Couples: A Content Analysis", *Journal of Marriage and the Family*, Vol. 39, pp. 323-30.

Herman, J.B. and Gyelstrom, K.K. (1977), "Working Men and Women: Inter- and Intra-role Conflict", *Psychology of Women Quarterly*, Vol. 1, pp. 319-33.

Hill, Reuben (1958), "Generic Features of Families Under Stress", *Social Casework*, Vol. 39, pp. 139-50.

Hiller, D.V. and Philliber, W.W. (1982), "Predicting Marital and Career Success Among Dual-Worker Couples", *Journal of Marriage and the Family*, Vol. 44, pp. 53-62.

Hochschild, A.R. with Machung, A. (1989), *The Second Shift: Working Parents and the Revolution at Home*, Viking: New York.

Hoffman, Lois (1977), "Changes in Family Roles, Socialization, and Sex Differences", *American Psychologist*, Vol. 32, pp. 644-57.

Holahan, C.K. and Gilbert, L.A. (1979), "Conflict Between Major Life Roles: Women and Men in Dual-career Couples", *Human Relations*, Vol. 32, pp. 451-67.

Holmstrom, Linda. (1972), *The Two-Career Family*, Schenkman Publishing: Cambridge, MA.

Huber, Joan. (1973), *Changing Women in a Changing Society*, University of Chicago Press: Chicago.

Hunt, Janet G. and Hunt, Larry L. (1982a), "The Dualities of Careers and Families: New Integrations or New Polarizations?" *Social Problems*, Vol. 29, No. 5, pp. 499-510.

Hunt, Janet G. and Hunt, Larry L. (1982b), "Dual-career Families: Vanguard of the Future or Residue of the Past?" in Aldous, Joan (ed.), *Two Paychecks: Life in Dual-earner Families*, Sage: Beverly Hills, CA.

Hughes, E.C. (1945), "Dilemmas and Contradictions of Status", *American Journal of Sociology*, Vol. 50, pp. 353-59.

Hymowitz, Carol (1984), "Women on Fast Track Try to Keep Their Careers and Children Separate", *Wall Street Journal*, September 19, p. 28.

James, William (1890), *Principles of Psychology*, Henry Holland and Co: New York.

Johnson, C.L. and Johnson, F.A. (1977), "Attitudes Toward Parenting in Dual-Career Families", *American Journal of Psychiatry*, Vol. 134, pp. 391-95.

Kahn, Robert L. and Cannell, Charles F. (1964), *The Dynamics of Interviewing*, John Wiley & Sons: New York.

Kantor, David and Lehr, William (1975), *Inside the Family: Toward a Theory of Family Process*, Harper Colophon Books: New York.

Kaplan, Abraham (1964), *The Conduct of Inquiry*, Chandler: San Francisco.

Keith, P.M. and Schafer, R.B. (1980), "Role Strain and Depression in Two Job Families", *Family Relations*, Vol. 29, pp. 483-88.

Kerlinger, Fred N. (1973), *Foundations of Behavioral Research*, Holt, Rinehart, and Winston: New York.

Killian, Lewis M. (1952), "The Significance of Multiple-Group Membership in Disaster", *American Journal of Sociology*, Vol. 57, pp. 309-14.

Klein, Susan Jean Ditchett (1975), "Chronic Kidney Disease: Impact on the Family and Strategies for Coping", unpublished doctoral dissertation, University of Minnesota: Minneapolis.

Koos, Earl L. (1946), *Families in Trouble*, Kings Crown Press: New York.

Levitan, Sar A. and Belous, Richard (1981), *What's Happening to the American Family*, Johns Hopkins University Press: Baltimore.

Marks, Stephen R. (1977), "Multiple Roles and Role Strain: Some Notes on Human Energy, Time, and Commitment", *American Sociological Review*, Vol. 42, pp. 921-36.

McCubbin, Hamilton I. (1979), "Integrating Coping Behavior in Family Stress Theory", *Journal of Marriage and the Family*, Vol. 42, No. 4, pp. 237-44.

McCubbin, H.I. and Patterson, J.M. (1981), "Family Stress Theory: The ABCX and Double ABCX Models", in McCubbin, H.I. and Patterson, J.M. (eds.), *Systematic Assessment of Family Stress and Coping: Tools for Research, Education, and Clinical Intervention*, University of Minnesota: Minneapolis, pp. 7-15.

McCubbin, Hamilton I. and Patterson, Joan M. (1980) "Family Stress, Coping and Social Support, Recent Research and Theory, An Expanded Version of Family Stress and Coping: A Decade Review", *Journal of Marriage and the Family*, Vol. 42, No. 4, pp. 855-71.

McNall, Scott G. and McNall, Sally A. (1983), *Plains Families: Exploring Sociology Through Social History*, St. Martin's Press: New York.

Mileti, Dennis S. (1985), "Role Conflict and Abandonment in Emergency Workers", *Emergency Management Review*, Vol. 2, No. 1, pp. 20-2.

Morris, Betsy (1984), "Single Parents Who Raise Children Feel Stretched Thin by Home, Job", *Wall Street Journal*, September 28, p. 31.

Nachimas, David and Nachimas, Chava (1981), *Research Methods in the Social Sciences*, St. Martin's Press: New York.

Nevill, D. and Damico, S. (1975), "Role Conflict in Women as a Function of Marital Status" *Human Relations*, Vol. 28, pp. 487-98.

Olson, D.H., McCubbin, H.I. et. al. (1983), "Family Coping Strategies", in Olson, D.H., McCubbin, H.I. et. al. (eds.), *Families: What Makes Them Work*, Sage: Beverly Hills, CA.

Otten, Alan L. (1986), "If you See Families Staging a Comeback, It's Probably a Mirage", *Wall Street Journal*, September 25, p. 1.

Park, Robert E. (1928), "Human Migration and the Marginal Man", *American Journal of Sociology*, Vol. 33, pp. 881-93.

Parsons, Talcott (1951), *The Social System*, The Free Press: Glencoe, IL.

Peak, Helen (1953), "Problems of Objective Observation", in Festinger, Leon and Katz, Daniel (eds.), *Research Methods in the Behavioral Sciences*, Dryden Press: New York.

Pearlin, Leonard and Schooler, Carmi (1978), "The Structure of Coping", *Journal of Health and Social Behavior*, Vol. 19, pp. 2-21.

Pendleton, B.F., Poloma, M.M. and Garland, T.N. (1980), "Scales for the Investigation of the Dual Career Family", *Journal of Marriage and the Family*, Vol. 42, pp. 269-76.

Poloma, Margaret M. (1972), "Role Conflict and the Married Professional Woman", in Safilios-Rothschild, Constantina (ed.), *Toward a Sociology of Women*, Xerox College Publishing: Lexington, MA, pp. 187-198.

Poloma, M.M. and Garland, T.N. (1971), "The Married Professional Woman: A Study in the Tolerance of Domestication", *Journal of Marriage and the Family*, Vol. 33, pp. 531-40.

Rapoport, R. and Rapoport, R. (1969), "The Dual-career Family: A Variant Pattern and Social Change", *Human Relations*, Vol. 22, pp. 3-30.

Rapoport, R. and Rapoport, R. (1971), "Further Considerations on the Dual Career Family", *Human Relations*, Vol. 24, pp. 519-33.

Rapoport, Rhona and Rapoport, Robert (1976), *Dual-career Families Re-examined: New Integrations of Work and Family*, Martin Robertson: London.

Rapoport, Rhona and Rapoport, Robert (1980), "Three Generations of Dual-Career Family Research", in Pepitone-Rockwell, Fran (ed.), *Dual-Career Couples*, Sage: Beverly Hills, CA, pp. 23-48.

Reiss, David and Oliveri, Mary Ellen (1980), "Family Paradigm and Family Coping: A Proposal for Linking the Family's Intrinsic Adaptive Capacities to its Responses to Stress", *Family Relations*, Vol. 29, pp. 431-44.

Roberts, Ted (1986), "Wife Studies Nursing and I Lose Patience", *Wall Street Journal*, September 16, p. 30.

Robinson, W.S. (1957), "The Statistical Measurement of Agreement", *American Sociological Review*, Vol. I, pp. 17-25.

Schwartz, Howard and Jacobs, Jerry (1979), *Qualitative Sociology: A Method to the Madness*, The Free Press: New York.

Sease, Douglas R. (1978), "Marital Relationships Undergo Strain When Wives get Jobs", *Wall Street Journal*, September 19, p.1.

Selltiz, Claire, Wrightsman, L.S. Wrightsman and Cook, S.W. (1976), *Research Methods in Social Relations*, Holt, Rinehart, & Winston: New York.

Sherif, Muzafer (1949), "The Problem of Inconsistency in Intergroup Relations", *Journal of Social Issues*, Vol. 5, pp. 32-7.

Skinner, D.A. (1980), "Dual Career Family Stress and Coping: A Literature Review", *Family Relations*, Vol. 29, pp. 473-80.

Slater, Philip (1970), *The Pursuit of Loneliness*, Beacon Press: Boston.

Slonim, Morris J. (1960), *Sampling*, Simon and Schuster: New York.

Spector, Paul E. (1981), *Research Designs*, Sage Publications: Beverly Hills, CA.

St. John-Parsons, D. (1978), "Continuous Dual-career Families: A Case Study", *Psychology of Women Quarterly*, Vol. 3, pp. 30-42.

Stanfield, Jacqueline B. (1985), "Research on Wife/mother Role Strain in Dual-career Families", *American Journal of Economics and Sociology*, Vol. 44, No. 3, pp. 355-63.

Stanfield, Jacqueline B. (1992), "Family Policy in America: A Continuing Controversy", *Review of Social Economy*, Vol. L, No. 4, pp. 420-31.

Starr, Paul D. (1977), "Marginality, Role Conflict, and Status Inconsistency as Forms of Stressful Interaction", *Human Relations*, Vol. 30, pp. 949-61.

Stewart, Charles J. and Cash, William B. (1974), *Interviewing: Principles and Practices*, William C. Brown: Dubuque, IA.

Stonequist, Everett (1937), *The Marginal Man*, Charles Scribner's Sons: New York.

Stouffer, Samuel A. and Toby, Jackson (1951), "Role Conflict and Personality", *American Journal of Sociology*, Vol. 56, pp. 395-406.

Sudman, Seymour (1965), "Time Allocation on Survey Interviewing and Other Field Occupations", *Public Opinion Quarterly*, Vol. 29, pp. 638-48.

Sutcliffe, J.P. and Haberman, M. (1956), "Factors Influencing Choice in Role Conflict Situations", *American Sociological Review*, Vol. 21, pp. 695-703.

US Bureau of the Census (1977), "Joint Labor Force and Employment Status of Husbands and Wives by Family Income: March 1977."

Current Population Reports, Series P-23, No. 77, U.S. Government Printing Office: Washington, D.C.

US Bureau of the Census (1984), "Earnings in 1981 of Married Couple Families, by Selected Characteristics", *Current Population Reports*, Series P-23, No. 133, U.S. Government Printing Office: Washington, D.C.

Vanek, Joann (1974), "Time Spent in Housework", *Scientific American*, November, pp. 116-120.

Venters, Maurine Henderson (1980), "Chronic Childhood Illness and Familial Coping: The Case of Cystic Fibrosis", unpublished doctoral dissertation, University of Minnesota: Minneapolis.

Weber, Max (1949 [1904]), "Objectivity in Social Science and Social Policy", in Shils, Edward A. and Finch, Henry A. (eds.), *The Methodology of the Social Sciences*, The Free Press of Glencoe: New York, pp. 89-94.

Weingarten, K. (1978), "The Employment Pattern of Professional Couples and their Distribution of Involvement in the Family", *Psychology of Women Quarterly*, Vol. 3, pp. 43-52.

Wessel, David (1984), "Working Fathers Feel New Pressure Arising from Child-Rearing Duties", *Wall Street Journal*, September 7, p. 27.

Whyte, William Foote (1943), *Street Corner Society*, University of Chicago Press: Chicago.

Yogev, S. (1981), "Do Professional Women Have Egalitarian Marital Relationships?", *Journal of Marriage and the Family*, Vol. 43, pp. 865-71.

Yorburg, Betty (1983), *Families and Societies: Survival or Extinction?*, Columbia University Press: New York.

Zimmerman, Shirley (1988), *Understanding Family Policy: Theoretical Approaches*, Sage Publications: Beverly Hills, California.

Census Population Reports, series P-21, No. 77, U.S. Government Printing Office, Washington, D.C.

US Bureau of the Census (1975), *Marriages in 1961, of Married Couples ... by Selected Characteristics ...*, Current Population Reports, Series P-20, No. 135, U.S. Government Printing Office, Washington, D.C.

Vanek, J. ... (1974), "Time Spent in Housework," *Scientific American*, November 1, pp.116-120.

Weinberg, Martha Henderson (1980), "Cultural Conflict in Illness and ... mental Therapy: the Case of the pain patients," unpublished doctoral dissertation, University of Milwaukee, Milwaukee.

Westergaard ... (19..), "Objectifying Social Science and Social Policy in Urban Theory," in ... Future Home ... , ... International Research Association, ... The Families of Children, New York, pp.3-34.

Whitehead ... (19..), "The Construction, Class and Educational Couples and their Distribution of Housework in the Family," *Sociology* ... , ... pp.9-27.

Wright ... (19..), "Women, Class and the New Feminine Mind," ... Administration Ideas," ... , ... , American Sociology, ... Oxford: Wright ... University of Oxford, ... Oxford.

Young ... (1975), "Do Housework Wives Have ... gain by Divorce," *Review and Study Journal of Marriage and the Family*, vol. 33, pp.33...